Copyright Notice

Strolling Around Rouen by Irene Reid

ISBN: 9798845967732

All rights reserved. This book may not be reproduced in any form, in whole or in part, without written permission from the author.

The author has made every effort to ensure the accuracy of the information in this book at the time of going to press, and cannot accept responsibility for any consequences arising from the use of the book.

Potted History

Friends! It is therefore Rouen, the city of old streets,
With old towers, debris of vanished races,
The city of a hundred bell towers ringing in the air,
The Rouen of castles, hotels, bastilles,
Whose front bristling with arrows and of needles
Incessantly tears the mists of the sea;

Victor Hugo, Autumn Leaves

Prehistory

Rouen lies on the Seine and the area has been inhabited for a very long time. Archaeologists have found tools and reindeer bones which are 35,000 years old, and ceramics from 6000 years ago.

The first inhabitants we can name were a tribe called the Veliocasses who settled there around 300 BC. They were conquered by Julius Caesar as he swept across Gaul.

The Romans

The Romans built on the right bank of the Seine as it lay high enough to avoid flooding, unlike the left bank which was marshy. They called the little town they founded Rotomagus and it became an important place in Roman Gaul as it lay between Paris and the sea.

Life was good for a few hundred years until the Roman Empire started to disintegrate. The Roman Empire split into two, the Eastern Empire ruled from Constantinople and the Western Empire ruled from Rome. Rouen became the principle city of Gaul in the Western Roman Empire.

The Franks and the Normans

The Western Roman Empire fell in 476 AD, as the tribes of northern Europe marched west and south. Northern Gaul was absorbed into the Frankish Empire which eventually stretched from France to Austria.

One area which the Franks failed to completely overpower was what we now call Normandy. It was constantly raided by the Vikings and lay in ruins. In the end, the only way to gain peace was to effectively give the land to the leader of the Vikings, as well as the King's daughter in marriage. It became the Duchy of Normandy with Rouen as its capital; the Viking leader Rollo became the first Duke of Normandy. He proved a very capable ruler and Normandy quickly became a powerhouse of Europe, both militarily and commercially.

Some generations later, William Duke of Normandy turned his attention to England. The English King Edward the Confessor died, and since he had no children, he left his kingdom to his brother-in-law Harold.

William and Edward happened to be cousins, so William considered he had more right to the crown than Harold. He crossed the channel in 1066, and defeated King Harold at the Battle of Hastings. The Norman Conquest of England was complete.

England thrown out of Normandy

However power comes and power goes, and in 1204 the French King conquered the Duchy of Normandy. He imposed some very unpopular taxes which eventually drove the poor of Rouen to rebel – they killed the mayor and ransacked the homes of the wealthy. An uneasy peace was eventually restored with Rouen remaining under the French crown.

The Hundred Years War and Joan

The scene was set. The Hundred Years' War was a long-running series of battles between England and France, each side claiming the French throne. The war actually lasted a bit longer than 100 years, from 1337 to 1453.

Rouen's most famous moment in that war involves the story of Joan of Arc.

The French King died leaving his son Charles, the Dauphin, to inherit the throne. Charles was just a child and ambitious factions in France tried to seize power from him. Meanwhile over in England, King Henry VI decided to reclaim the French crown once more, and managed to capture parts of Normandy.

The Dauphin came of age during this long conflict. By tradition, the coronation of the French King had to take place in Reims Cathedral. However Reims was held by the Dauphin's enemies, meaning he could not be crowned.

Joan was a peasant girl. She started to hear voices from God which instructed her to help the Dauphin defeat the armies of England and their allies the Burgundians, and to see him crowned King of France in Reims.

At first no-one took her seriously, but eventually she was given an army and sent to break the siege of Orleans. With the help of the voices, Joan managed to rally her troops and break the siege. She was immediately proclaimed The Maid of Orleans and her fame spread.

She battled on and defeated the English army before finally taking the Dauphin to Reims where he was crowned.

Joan was eventually captured by her enemies and imprisoned in Rouen. She was charged with heresy and witchcraft, and she was burned at the stake in Rouen at just nineteen.

Rouen eventually fell to the French in 1449 as the Hundred Years War drew to an end.

Wars of Religion and Decline

However war soon returned - this time over religion.

France had both Huguenot (protestant) citizens and Catholic citizens. They fought for over thirty years at the end of the sixteenth century, and Rouen was one of the battlegrounds. Not surprisingly people fled, and Rouen fell into decline

Modern Rouen

Rouen only started to recover economically in the nineteenth century when the textile industry arrived. Rouen had plenty of wool and water to make use of, and looms were soon producing high quality cloths such as linen.

These days the old city survives on the tourist industry, while the outer city is full of modern-day businesses and service industries.

The Stars

Gustave Flaubert

Flaubert was an author from Rouen. He wrote about life in Normandy during the mid-nineteenth century, and sometimes his portrayal of Norman life was a bit too close to reality for general approval.

His most famous/infamous novel was his first, Madame Bovary. It tells the story of a Emma Bovary, a doctor's wife who is utterly bored with her life. She embarks on an adventure of lust and luxury.

When it was published it caused an uproar. Flaubert was accused of obscenity and taken to court. He was acquitted, but the huge publicity generated by the trial made him and his book famous. As might be expected, it became a bestseller – not the outcome his accusers had hoped for. The novel is now regarded as a masterpiece.

Pierre Corneille

He was a writer from the seventeenth century, and his most famous work was the play Le Cid.

At that time there were strict rules on the structure and content of plays in France, which Corneille just ignored. This led to a long battle with the authorities who guarded French culture; the battle became known as The Quarrel of Le Cid.

The Académie Française investigated the matter and declared Le Cid broke too many of the rules. At that point Corneille retired, and when he resurfaced some years later his plays stuck much more rigidly to the "rules".

However Le Cid has stayed popular to the present day, and was made into a Hollywood movie starring Charlton Heston and Sophia Loren. The name changed slightly to El Cid.

The Walks

There are four walks to try to fit in, but if time is short do try to do cover Walk 1 and Walk 2.

However the walks do actually link up, starting and ending at the Old Market Square. So you could start at walk 1 and just keep going, trying to cover as much ground as possible.

Walk 1 – Joan and a Clock

This walk takes you around the Old Market Square of Rouen, then through the old town to reach the Cathedral square.

Walk 2 – The Cathedral to Saint Maclou

This walk explores the Cathedral, then takes you to the Saint Maclou church and its macabre graveyard.

Walk 3 – A River Walk to the Abbey

This walk starts from the Saint Maclou church and takes you along one the prettiest streets in Rouen, before turning north to reach Rouen's famous abbey.

Walk 4 – Town Hall and the Museums

This walk takes you from the Abbey to the museum district, then turns south again to return you to the Old Market Square.

Get Ready

Opening hours are always a problem when exploring a city. Take note of the following.

Musée des Beaux-Arts

This museum is closed on Tuesdays.

If you enjoy art, expect to spend a couple of hours there, so plan accordingly. Entrance is free

The Sublime House

Walk 1 takes you past the Palais de Justice. If you would like to visit The Sublime House which is in its grounds, you will need to visit on a Saturday. The website is:

https://www.visitezlamaisonsublime.fr/en/tours/guided-tours/

Saint Maclou

This church is only open on Monday, Saturday, and Sunday.

Pierre Corneille

This little museum is open in the afternoons Tuesday to Sunday.

Saint Ouen Abbey

At the moment the Abbey is closed for an extensive restoration project.

Musée Le Secq des Tournelles

This little museum is closed on Tuesdays.

Ceramics Museum

This museum is closed on Tuesdays.

Sails of Liberty

To celebrate the bicentenary of the French Revolution in 1989, it was decided to invite the world's largest sailing ships to Rouen.

That event was a great success, and it is now repeated every four to six years. The visiting invitation list has expanded and now includes warships, submarines, and all sorts of other great vessels.

At the time of writing, the next gathering is planned for 2027.

The Maps

There are maps sprinkled all through the walks to help you find your way. If you need to check where you are at any point during a walk, always flip back to find the map you need.

To help you follow the maps, each map shows its start point. In addition numbered directions have been placed on each map. The numbers correspond to the directions within the walks.

Walk 1 – Joan and a Clock

This walk takes you from the Old Market Square to the famous Big Clock, and then to Cathedral Square.

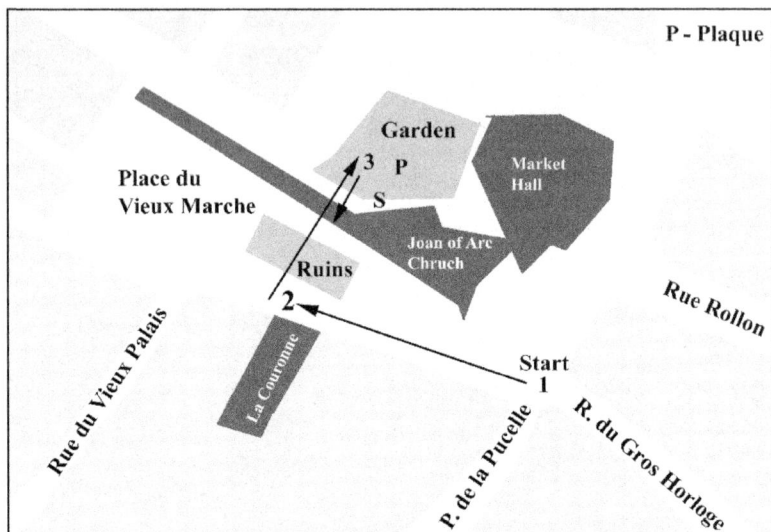

Map 1

The walk starts in Place du Vieux Marche, on the corner of Place de la Pucelle and Rue du Gros Horloge in the southeast corner.

Place du Vieux Marche

The square's name means the Old Market Square, and it has been in use since medieval times.

It is surrounded by a mixture of pleasant half-timbered buildings and more modern buildings which were put up after the bombardments of World War II.

After the war Rouen decided to restore the market. They also decided to construct a new church to replace an ancient church which had been damaged and later destroyed during the French Revolution in the eighteenth century.

From the corner where you are standing, you can see the results. The new Sainte Jeanne d'Arc church dominates the square in the centre, and the new Market Hall which sits just beside the church.

If you visit in the evening you will find it full of people sitting outside the many bars and restaurants enjoying a drink and the evening.

Market Hall

The Market Hall with its peaked roofs reflects the architectural style of the new church.

Opinion is divided, but on a personal note the Market Hall seems to spoil the entire square. If the Market Hall and its accompanying vans, cars, pallets, and other market detritus were removed and replaced with gardens, the whole square would be much pleasanter.

However, inside you will find a really good food market, where all sorts of interesting eatables are on display, especially seafood. There's even an oyster bar. So you might want to visit for a look around.

Map 1.1 – Stand at the corner of Place de la Pucelle and Rue du Gros Horloge. Walk along the left-hand side of the square, keeping the Joan of Arc church on your right.

Pause when you see a restaurant called La Couronne on your left. It sits at number 29 and it usually has many flags and flowers decorating it.

La Couronne

It claims to be the oldest auberge in France, opening in 1345. It specialises in French and Norman specialities.

It became very popular with Hollywood stars and artists. If you venture in you can see signed pictures around the walls, Salvador Dali, John Wayne, Josephine Baker, Brigitte Bardot, Audrey Hepburn, Gene Kelly, and many others.

Julia Child

You may have enjoyed the movie "Julie and Julia" which tells how American Julia Child became a chef after she discovered the delights of French gastronomy.

It's said that it was in La Couronne that she tasted her first French meal. Her life changed forever as she brought French gastronomy to the USA. In her memoirs she wrote:

> Rouen is famous for its duck dishes, but after consulting the waiter, Paul decided to order sole Meuniére.
>
> It arrived whole: a large, flat Dover sole that was perfectly browned in a sputtering butter sauce with a sprinkling of chopped parsley on top. The waiter carefully placed the platter in front of us, stepped back, and said: "bon appétit!"
>
> I closed my eyes and inhaled the rising perfume. Then I lifted a forkful of fish in my mouth, took a bite, and chewed slowly. The flesh of the sole was delicate, with a light but distinct taste of the ocean that blended marvellously with the browned butter. I chewed slowly and swallowed. It was a morsel of perfection

If you can fit dinner into your schedule and don't mind the price, you could order "Julia Child's Menu" in La Couronne.

Just outside the auberge lies all that remains of a very old church.

Saint-Sauveur du Marché

The ruins you see now were uncovered when the square was renovated in the 1970's. The experts have dated some of the oldest foundation stones from the 11th century, and have identified scorch marks left from the fire which destroyed that first church.

The church was rebuilt more than once over the centuries, but it was finally closed and later demolished after the French Revolution.

The stones which the old church was built from were valuable and were sold. However the church altar was not and it was unearthed during the excavations in the 1970s.

You will probably find other tourists sitting on the ruins. It's a poignant spot.

Église Sainte-Jeanne-d'Arc

Also from outside the auberge, you can see the full length of the Joan of Arc Church and the odd shape of its roof. The roof is meant to look like an upturned long-ship; a link to Normandy's Viking past.

Its construction was kicked off by President Giscard d'Estaing in 1979. Its very modern design and style caused a lot of discussion and criticism; however Rouen has got used to it.

Map 1.2 - Before going into the Joan of Arc church, walk straight ahead to pass under its long elevated roof.

Joan of Arc Plaque

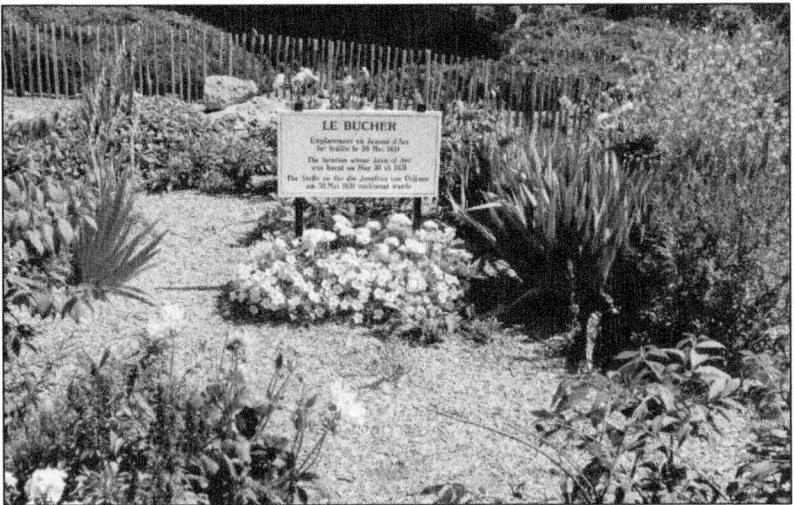

Once through, look to your right to find a little garden. This area was often used for public executions.

Spot the plaque which marks the exact spot where Jeanne d'Arc burned for her beliefs. It is titled "Le Bucher" (The Pyre).

The authorities of the time were absolutely determined that Joan would not become a martyr, so her ashes were gathered up and tossed into the River Seine, leaving not a single trace.

Behind the little garden and against the church wall is a touching statue of Joan at the stake. You can see the flames beginning to burn her robe.

This statue was made in 1929. It was sculpted by Maxime Real del Sarte who was a great admirer of Joan. He fought in World War I and lost an arm, but continued to sculpt.

Map 1.3 - Make your way to the church entrance and enter. If you do not want to visit the church, continue from "Leaving the Church" on page 21.

Inside the church

The Windows

You will be immediately struck by the wonderful stained glass windows on your left-hand side. So descend the steps and find a seat and take them in.

The thirteen windows are from the old St Vincent church which once stood near the Siene but which was destroyed in 1944 by bombing raids. Thankfully the beautiful windows had been removed to safety in 1939.

When the new Joan of Arc church was planned, it seemed the perfect place to restore them into.

Let's number the windows from 1 to 13, with number 1 nearest the church entrance. Note, it might look like there are only 12 windows, but two of them are smaller than the other 11 and are positioned one above the other.

The windows illustrate the following biblical characters and events:

St. Peter
St. Anne
The Virgin's Triumph
St. Anne's Tree
The life of St. John the Baptist
The Works of mercy
St. Anthony of Padua
The Saints
The childhood and public life of Christ
The Passion
The Crucifixion
The glorious life of Christ
The martyrdom of St. Vincent

Fishy Secrets

Don't miss the large windows opposite the stained glass windows. They are modern and much less eye-catching but still interesting because of their fish-shape.

Back in Roman times when Christians were being persecuted, the fish was adopted as a symbol of recognition between Christians. The Greek word for fish is "ichthys" and it was taken as an acrostic of Iesous Christos Theou Yios Soter, i.e. Jesus Christ, Son of God, Savior. So throughout history, the fish has been a symbol of Christianity.

The Roof

The roof is certainly very impressive. It does look like a huge upturned Viking ship, with its curved wooden beams forming the hull of the ship.

Joan

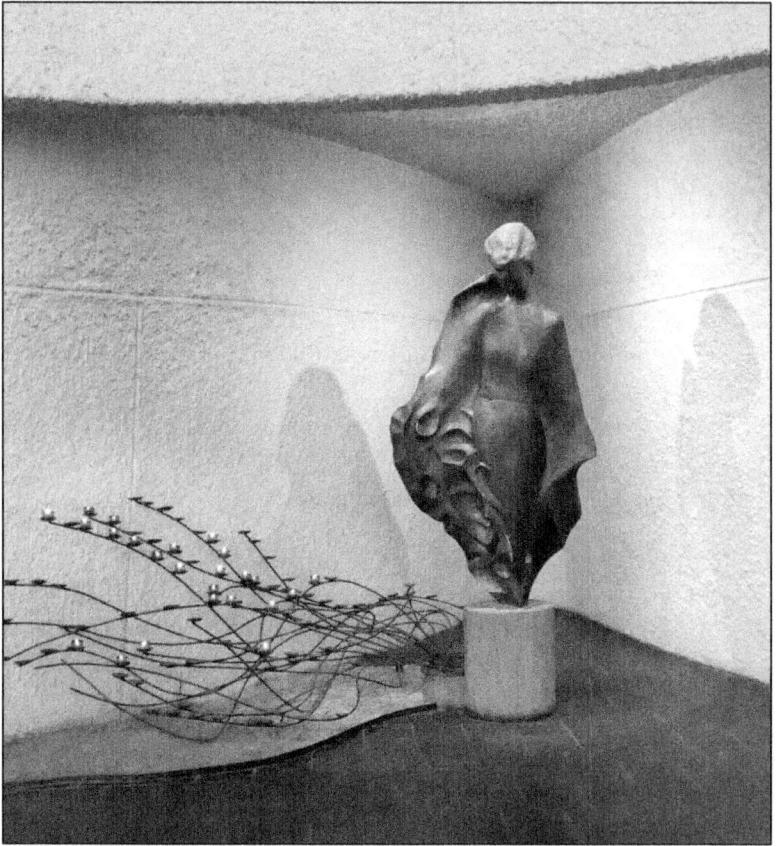

Find the sanctuary of St Joan of Arc – it sits in the furthest corner from the entrance. There you will find another poignant statue of Joan, obeying the voices from God and burning in the flames.

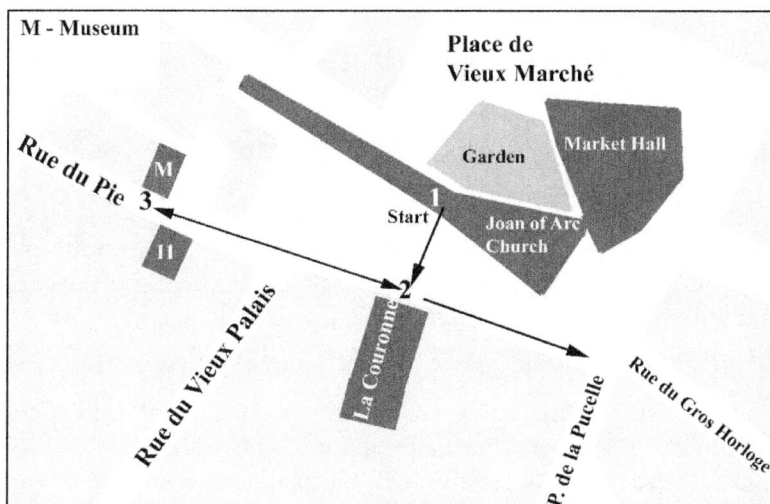

Map 2

Leaving the Church

Map 2.1 – When you have seen enough, exit the church and return to the front of La Couronne.

Map 2.2 - Face the restaurant and turn right to walk to the end of the square.

Walk straight ahead into Rue du Pie as far as number 11 on your left-hand side. A few more steps will bring you to a half-timbered house with stained glass windows on your right.

Pierre Corneille

That is the house where Pierre Corneille was born and lived in the seventeenth century. Since it's free you could pop in for a quick look.

Corneille is thought to be one of France's greatest playwrights. He was baptised in the Saint-Sauveur du Marché church, the ruins of which you have just seen.

His most famous work is El Cid, which was based on the life of Rodrigo Díaz de Vivar, a knight from Castile in Spain.

When the play was first published it caused Corneille a lot of trouble with the French authorities. At the time Cardinal Richelieu had imposed strict rules on theatre and literature which seem quite bizarre to us now.

For instance his rules stated that a play must take place within a single day, must have just one setting, and must have just one story arc. Corneille's El Cid broke most of Richelieu's rules, and after a lot of arguing Corneille gave up writing for years.

However El Cid survived and was later made into a film, starring Charlton Heston as El Cid and Sophia Loren as his wife.

If you do go inside the museum, you will see a reconstruction of Corneille's study and a collection of his works.

Map 2.3 – With the door of the museum behind you, turn left to return to La Couronne.

Walk straight ahead along the right-hand side of the square keeping the Joan of Arc church on your left.

You will return to the corner of Place de la Pucelle and Rue du Gros Horloge.

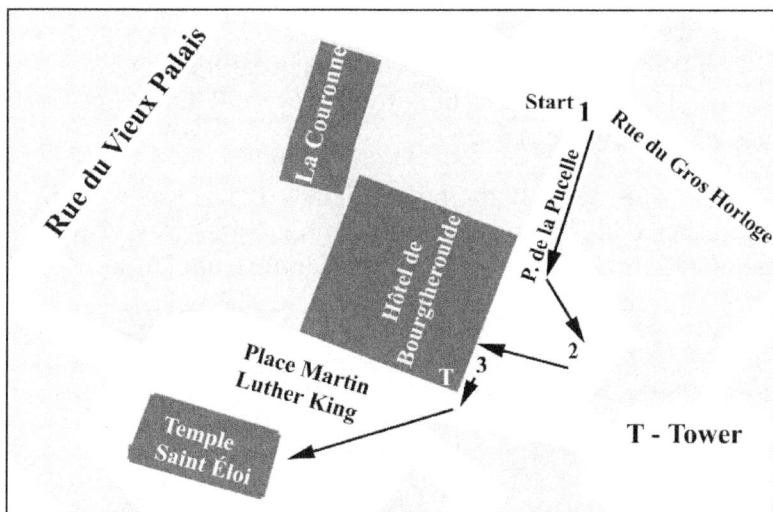

Map 3

Map 3.1 - Turn right and walk along Place de la Pucelle. It leads into a nice square which has a little garden in it.

Walk into the centre of the square.

Place de la Pucelle (Place of the Maid).

For many years this square was thought to be where Joan of Arc was burned at the stake, but that was incorrect.

At one time there was a fountain here dedicated to Joan, but it was destroyed in WWII and sadly never replaced.

Turn right to see the Hôtel de Bourgtheroulde on the corner of the square. It has a pretty corner turret and an ornately sculpted facade.

Hôtel de Bourgtheroulde

Beautiful stone mansions were essential for ambitious and powerful men; they were built to impress and house important visitors and business partners.

This one was built by William II Le Roux, lord of Bourgtheroulde in the fifteenth century, and was visited by members of the all-powerful Medici family from Florence.

The ornate entrance is topped by two leopards holding up the arms of the Bourgtheroulde family.

To the right of the leopards you can see a very spiky porcupine topped by a crown. That was the symbol of King Louis XII.

The building was devastated in World War II but has been beautifully restored, although not to its former opulence. It first became a bank but is now a luxury hotel.

Map 3.2 - If you have time, pop into its gorgeous courtyard for a look around. You could stop for a coffee while you're there if inclined.

The Courtyard

The Le Roux family had the left-hand side of the courtyard decorated with limestone bas-reliefs.

Triumphs of Petrarch

The top row shows us the Triumphs of Petrarch, a series of poems by Petrarch who was a famous scholar from the fourteenth century.

Each depicted triumph shows a Roman style Triumphal procession. Rather than being led by a victorious Roman General, the procession is led by Love, Chastity, Death, Fame, Time, and Eternity.

The Field of Cloth of Gold.

The bottom row displays scenes from the famous "Field of Cloth of Gold" meeting. It was basically an eighteen day confab between King Henry VIII of England and Francois I of France near Calais. Naturally each king was accompanied by many important members of court.

The first panel on the left shows King Henry and his court riding to the meeting place.

The second panel shows Cardinal Wolsey, who engineered the meeting. He is just left of centre wearing a flat hat and preceded by a courtier carrying a simple cross.

The third panel shows the two kings meeting.

The fourth panel shows Cardinal de Boissy, the counterpart of Cardinal Wolsey. He is preceded by a courtier carrying a much more complex cross. The point being that Cardinal Boissy was more important that Cardinal Wolsey

Finally the fourth panel shows the French King and his court on their way to the meeting.

The money which was spent on the venue was eye-watering, and despite everyone who attended having a wonderful time, nothing of importance was actually agreed between France and England.

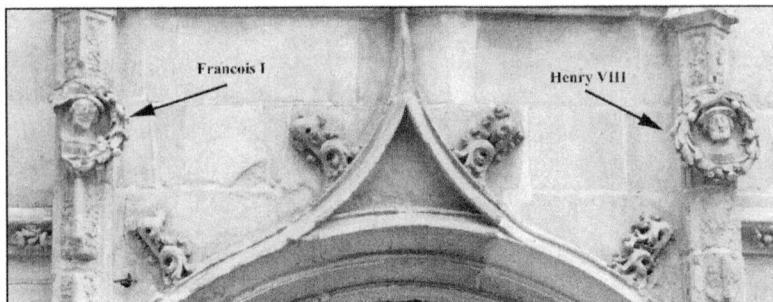

If you turn to have a look at the archway you entered by, notice the two medallions on either side. These are thought to be King Francois I and King Henry VIII.

On a literary note, its thought that Flaubert had this beautiful building in mind as the Hôtel de Boulogne where he had Madame Bovary meet her lover.

Note, if you are in town in the evening and a cocktail takes your fancy, you could splash out and visit the Art Deco cocktail bar in this hotel.

Exit the courtyard.

Map 3.3 - When you are ready to move on, face the hotel and walk round its left-hand side into Place Martin Luther King.

You will see the now rather neglected Temple Saint-Éloi.

Temple Saint Éloi

The first church which stood on this site was built in the eleventh century. It stood on an island in the river Seine, so you can see just how far the river has shifted south over the centuries. The Seine now lies about 300 metres to the south.

This impressive but now rather uncared for church, was built during the sixteenth century, during the Wars of Religion.

That was another tragic period of French history. The French Catholics and Protestants went to war because of their beliefs, and those good Christians indulged in riots, battles, and massacres. The church was sacked by the Huguenots (the Protestants) during the Siege of Rouen, when Rouen's Protestants attacked many religious buildings.

The church was rebuilt when peace settled, but its luck ran out again after the French Revolution; it was closed and became a lead factory and then used for grain storage.

When Napoleon took power, he restored it as a church and ironically it was given to the Protestants.

It was damaged in WWII but was restored once more in 1950. During that restoration, the excavators unearthed pieces of statues which had been attacked during the Siege of Rouen, and they are now in a museum.

The church is not open very often. If you feel inclined to walk round it, you might spot posters for organ concerts which are sometimes held here.

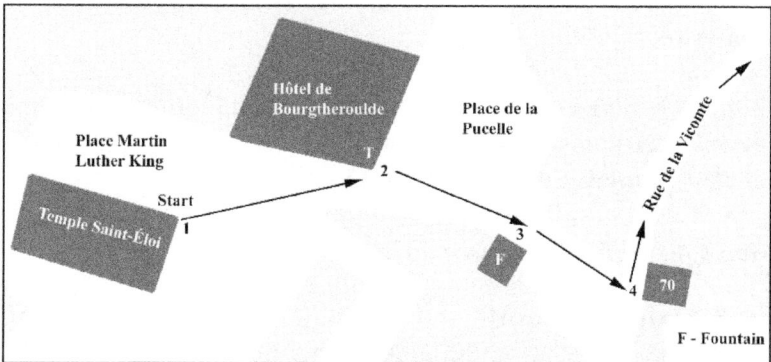

Map 4

Map 4.1 – Backtrack to the corner of Place de la Pucelle and re-enter the square.

Map 4.2 – Stand with the Hôtel de Bourgtheroulde's little turret directly behind you.

Walk straight ahead along the square's right-hand side. As you reach the other corner of the square, you will find a modern building on your right-hand side.

Gallo-Romain Fountain

The building itself is of absolutely no interest. However look through the ground-floor window and you should be able to see the basin of an ancient water fountain from 2000 years ago. It's a very rare example of Rouen's Roman history. It was discovered when a car park was being installed beneath Place de la Pucelle.

The company which is currently in residence allows the public to enter to have a closer look at the fountain. The door is to the right of the window, so if it's open you could take a closer look. You can also see a pillar which was found at the same site.

Map 4.3 – When you want to move on, stand with the fountain window on your right-hand side. Continue straight ahead to reach a T-junction with Rue de la Vicomte.

Map 4.4 - Turn left into Rue de la Vicomte

70 Rue de la Vicomte

This is another street lined with more of Rouen's half-timbered houses.

Number 70 Rue de la Vicomte on your right, is especially nice with its colourful decoration above the first floor.

Continue to reach a crossroads with Rue du Gros Horloge.

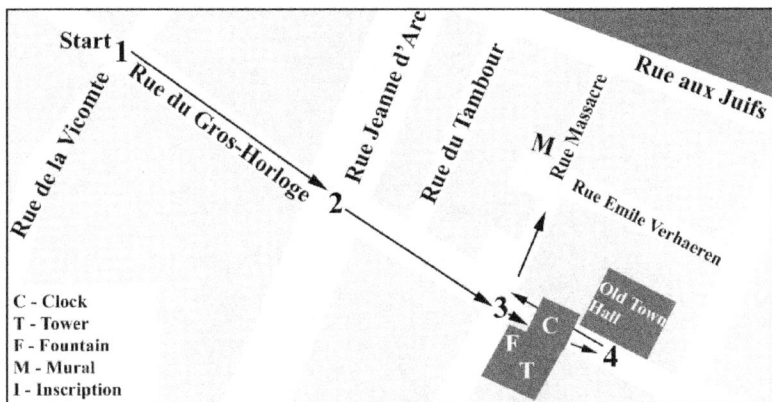

Map 5

Map 5.1 – Turn Right into Rue du Gros Horloge.

You will see one of Rouen's most iconic sights ahead of you - the golden Big Clock so walk towards it.

You will reach a crossroads with busy Rue Jeanne d'Arc.

Map 5.2 - Carefully cross Rue Jeanne d'Arc. Continue towards the clock passing Rue du Tambour on your left. Pause when you reach the clock.

Le Gros Horloge

The clock mechanism was constructed in the fourteenth century. It and a set of bells, which were the first in Rouen which did not belong to a church, were placed in the gothic tower you see on your right.

At that time the clock didn't have a clock-face, its job was to keep time and the bells pealed out as needed.

A hundred or so years later the clock was removed from the tower and placed in its current location. At the same time the ornate clock façade was added. The bells stayed in the belfry and are still driven by the clock – although the clock is itself now electric!

The clock dial is marked out by 24 sun-rays, and the hour hand moves round them as the day progresses. There was no need for a minute hand as people did not fret so much about timekeeping in those days – what was five minutes!

Wool was the most important industry in Rouen at the time, so there are many golden sheep to be spotted.

Spot the sphere above the dial which rotates to match the phases of the moon.

A lovely touch sits beneath the clock; it shows the day of the week by depicting a god or goddess in a chariot:

Monday – Diana
Tuesday – Mars
Wednesday - Mercury
Thursday - Jupiter
Friday - Venus
Saturday - Saturn
Sunday – Apollo

The Archway

The archway is decorated with Rouen's coat of arms held up by two angels. Beneath that and running around the archway is a sequence of little cherub heads.

One of them is upside-down. Apparently there was a dispute over wages between the stone carvers and the city rulers when the unfortunate cherub was being carved!

Note, you can visit both the tower and the inside of the clock itself to see the ancient clock mechanism. The entrance is at the foot of the tower.

On your left-hand side and at the base of the tower stands a wonderful old fountain.

Horloge Fountain

At the time of writing it is not actually working which is a shame.

The first fountain was built here in the thirteenth century and was called the Massacre Fountain after the Massacre Gate which once stood here. This version was built in 1733.

Alpheus and Arethuse

The figures on the fountain represent Alpheus a river god, and Arethuse a sea nymph.

Arethuse decided one day to leave the sea and bathe in a stream. She was spotted by Alpheus who instantly fell in love with her. Arethuse was having none of it, scarpered and prayed to the other gods for help.

Artemis tried to help and turned her into a spring in Ortygia, a tiny island just off Sicily. The river god refused to give up and tunnelled under the Mediterranean to reach the spring and flow into it – a typical Greek myth euphemism for rape or seduction.

The river Alpheus in Sicily does flow underground at one point, and long ago it was believed that if you dropped a flower into the river, it would pop up in the spring.

Under the Archway

Map 5.3 - Take a few steps under the archway

As you do, look up to see some incredibly intricate carving. Jesus is there as the Good Shepherd, and he is surrounded by lots of sheep.

Take a few steps further along Rue du Gros Horloge.

The Old Town Hall

You will see a huge stone building with a central archway on your left-hand side. That is what is left of the Town Hall which was first built on this site in the thirteenth century.

It was expanded several times over the centuries, as Rouen grew in power and wealth. After the French Revolution it was decided to build a much larger Town Hall. You will see it if you manage to fit Walk 4 into your schedule.

The old Town Hall was sold off, and a lot of it has since disappeared, leaving just this impressive building.

Map 5.4 – Backtrack to walk under the archway once more. Take the first right into Rue Massacre.

Rue Massacre

The massacre in question had nothing to do with war; many butchers dispatched their livestock in this street before sending them to market!

Rue Massacre narrows and but then opens out again as you reach Rue Emile Verhaeren on your right.

This little area has just recently been named Place Dominique Laboubee.

Laboubee

You will see a mural of Laboubee on the wall.

Laboubee was a composer and singer in a Normandy rock group called Les Dogs which was formed in Rouen in 1973.

They were on tour in the USA in 2002 even through Laboubee was suffering from cancer. At a gig in Massachusetts he only managed one song before collapsing on stage, and being rushed to hospital where he died.

A little record store called Melodies Massacre sat on this square. Its owner was the band's manager, and Les Dogs recorded their first record in his cellar in the 1970's.

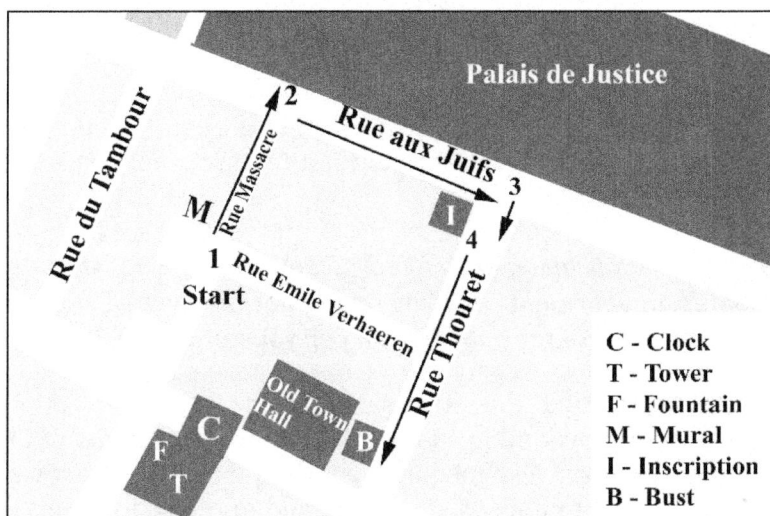

Map 6.1 – Continue straight ahead along Rue Massacre. At its end turn right into Rue aux Juifs – the street of the Jews.

Rouen's Jewish community

This area was where Rouen's Jewish community once worked and lived. This was the main street and it was called Vicus Judaeorum (The village of the Jews) in the Middle Ages.

Rouen's Jewish Community lived peacefully in Rouen until the start of The Crusades in the eleventh century. The "fight for the holy land" led to distrust between Rouen's Christians and Jews, and as always seemed to be the case, many Jews were attacked, murdered, or impoverished.

The Jewish community's fortunes waxed and waned depending on the mood of the people, the crown, and the church. E.g. in 1307 King Philip IV expelled the Jews from France altogether, mainly because he owed them vast amounts of money.

Finally the Jews had to face the horrors of Nazi Germany. It's thought 25% of France's Jewish population were taken to the concentration camps and never returned.

There is however still a Jewish community in Rouen, and a modern synagogue has been built not too far from where you are standing.

Map 6.2 – Walk along Rue aux Juifs. Pause when you reach Rue Thouret on your right. It's where you get the best view of the Palais de Justice – the huge building on your left.

Palais de Justice

The enormous Gothic building was started at the end of the fifteenth century. The medieval Jewish quarter of Rouen was knocked down to make space for it, and only the street name survived.

The Normandy Parliament once sat in this building. It only became the city's courthouse after the French Revolution.

Like a lot of Rouen's lovely buildings it was largely destroyed by allied bombing, but as you can see it has been carefully restored.

The central turret in the courtyard is especially lovely. Above it and running the length of the building is a line of statues. They represent people from all parts of society, from King Louis XII and Cardinal d'Amboise, to a villager and a farmer.

A tour of the Court House is available, but at the time of writing only once a week on Tuesdays. So this needs pre-booking and planning at the tourist office.

The Sublime House

In 1976 the ground floor of a small building was discovered beneath a staircase in the east wing of the Palais de Justice. Historians think it was a school for Jewish studies.

An inscription was found on a wall:

May this house be always sublime

It can now be visited but currently only on Saturdays.

Map 6.3 - With the Courthouse courtyard behind you, walk straight ahead to take a few steps into Rue Thouret.

Rue Thouret

On your right-hand side as you enter Rue Thouret, you will find an inscription protected by a glass panel. It sits just below the street-name.

This area was blasted by the allies in WWII, and that devastation is marked by an anonymous inscription on the wall:

Détruit par les libérateurs
Destroyed by the liberators

Map 6.3 - Continue along Rue Thouret. As you reach the end you will see a bust of Jacques Guillaume Thouret himself above a doorway on your right.

Jacques Guillaume Thouret

Thouret was a lawyer from Rouen, who opposed the church and supported the French Revolution.

The new French Government gave him the task of splitting France up into its many Departments. His first attempt was not too impressive - he split the country into 80 departments by simply laying a square grid over the map of France. If adopted it would have resulted in arbitrarily splitting towns, farms, bridges etc.

Common sense prevailed thank goodness, and his scheme was quietly modified into today's departments which are based on sensible geographical boundaries.

Thouret later made a serious political error by becoming a member of the Girondins. They were a political group which fell out of favour with the revolutionary high command, and paid the ultimate price. Thouret lost his head to the guillotine.

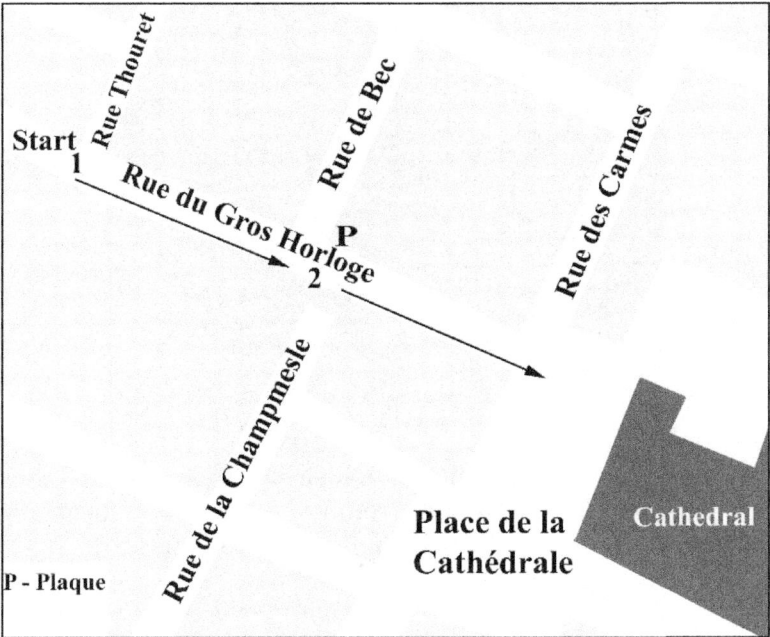

Map 7

Map 7.1 - Turn left into Rue du Gros Horloge once more.

Rue du Gros Horloge

This lovely pedestrianised street is lined with half-timbered houses. Rouen has about 2000 of these elderly buildings and some date back as far as Joan of Arc's time. Rouen stopped building them in 1520 as they were seen quite rightly as a fire risk.

Pause when you reach Rue du Bec, the next street on your left.

Robert Cavelier de la Salle

SUR LA PAROISSE SAINT-HERBLAND
S'ELEVAIT LA MAISON OU NAQUIT
LE 22 NOVEMBRE 1643
ROBERT CAVELIER DE LA SALLE

On the corner is a plaque which commemorates Robert Cavelier de la Salle who came from Rouen. It shows his profile flanked on either side with profiles of Native Americans.

He successfully explored the Great Lakes in Canada and a huge part of the USA. He later sailed down the Mississippi and claimed the territory of Louisiana for France.

He wasn't so lucky on his last expedition which tried to found a settlement. His expedition was attacked both at sea and on land, losing both ships and men. They did manage to found a settlement in what is now Texas, but de la Salle was later murdered by one of the settlers. The settlement didn't survive, as it was soon attacked by Native Americans and lost.

Map 7.2 - With Rue du Bec on your left, you will see the Cathedral straight ahead of you. Walk straight towards it into Place de la Cathedrale.

You have now reached the end of this walk. You could continue with Walk 2 which starts from this point.

Walk 2 - The Cathedral to Saint Maclou

This walk first takes you into the Cathedral. You then head towards the Saint Maclou Church and its macabre graveyard.

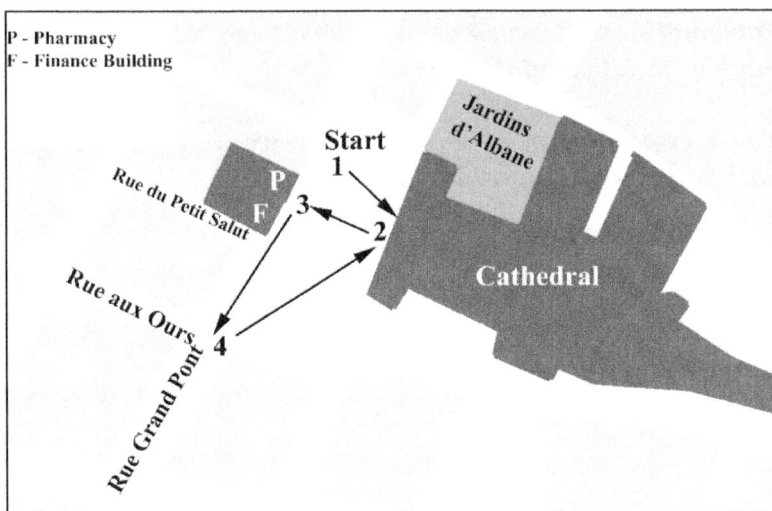

Map 1

This walk starts in front of the Cathedral in Place de la Cathedrale.

Place de la Cathédrale

It's a shame that the square on this side of the cathedral really doesn't do it justice. It's mostly bordered by relatively modern buildings and rather uninteresting shops.

Way back in the sixteenth century, the square was paved and walled, and there was a stone cross at both ends. Both the walls and the crosses disappeared during the revolution, and many of the interesting buildings which surrounded the square were lost in WWII.

So try to ignore the square's current rather bland appearance. Stand well back to take a good look at the Cathedral.

Note, if you are here in summer, you should return in the evening to watch the Cathedral of Lights show.

The Cathedral

The first religious building on this site went up in the fourth century, and it was replaced many times over the centuries in various styles.

It turned into a Romanesque Cathedral in the eleventh century. It was consecrated by William the Duke of Normandy, aka William the Conqueror, just before he hopped over the channel to invade England.

The Cathedral was then added to and altered repeatedly over the centuries. It emerged as a Gothic Cathedral in the thirteenth century, after a huge fire saw off a lot of the previous Romanesque construction.

It was attacked by the Huguenots in the Wars of Religion, but managed to survive more or less intact.

However World War II devastated it and a massive restoration had to take place. The façade has recently emerged from scaffolding following its restoration and much needed cleaning.

The Towers

Work on the left hand tower started in the twelfth century and the right hand tower was completed in the sixteenth.

Between the two towers but set back a bit, soars the slim pointed Lantern Tower.

Between the two front towers is a sculpted montage of biblical and historical characters.

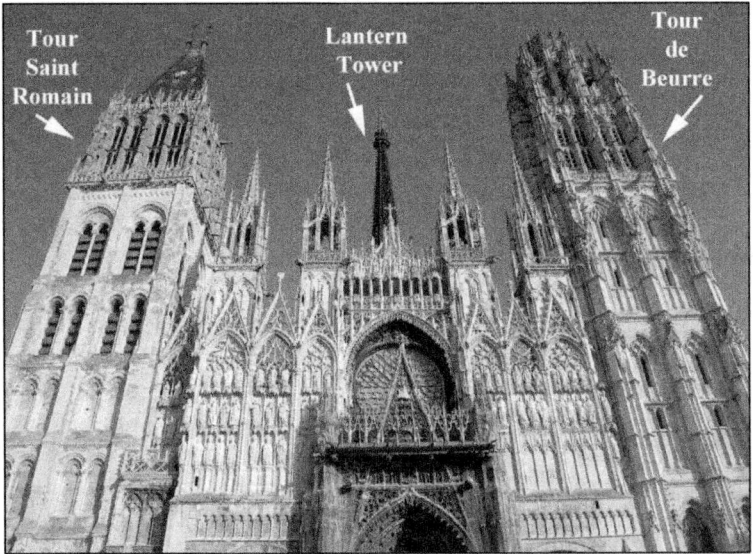

Tour St Romain
The left hand tower is the oldest part of the cathedral and was begun in 1145. It suffered greatly during WWII after allied bombing left only the walls standing - the heat was so intense that the bells melted.

Tour de Beurre
There are two theories on how the tower on the right got such a name. The first is simply that the tower was built using a yellowish limestone stone which differs from the rest of the church.

The second explanation is to do with Lent when butter was one of the luxuries which were banned. People with enough money could buy their way out of that rule by making a donation to the church. The funds gathered were used to pay for the tower.

As already mentioned the church took a very long time to build. By the time they got around to finishing the tower, styles had changed. That is why the cathedral has a lantern tower rather than the more traditional gothic spire. The tower is however still flamboyantly gothic, decorated with gables and gargoyles.

The Bells

The bell-makers got to work at the start of the fifteenth century. They cast a bell which was ten feet high, and it was named George d'Amboise after the bishop who commissioned it.

The King of France visited Rouen in 1786 and George d'Amboise was rung so hard in celebration that it cracked. It never got repaired as the French Revolution erupted. Instead it was melted down and turned into cannons and a few medals which were inscribed with:

Monument de vanité
Détruit pour l'utilité
L'an deux de l'égalité
Monument of vanity,
Destroyed for utility,
The second year of Equality

Joan of Arc

A new bell, which weighed in at sixteen tons, was installed in 1920. It was named the Joan of Arc. However in 1944 the Saint Romain tower caught fire from allied bombing, and the intense heat melted the bells which crashed to the ground. So just like its namesake, the Joan of Arc bell perished in the flames.

In 1954 a new Joan of Arc was cast and installed in the Cathedral once more. This version weighs in at 10 tons.

Lantern Tower

Because of its recessed position, this tall central tower doesn't stand out as much as it should, and it's difficult to appreciate its height.

The Lantern Tower has a history of burning, either through negligence or lightning. This incarnation went up in the nineteenth century after another fatal lightning strike.

The tower made the cathedral the tallest building in the world from 1876 to 1880, when Cologne's Cathedral stole that glory. It is still the fourth tallest church building in the world, and the tallest in France.

The Statues

Between the two towers are 70 large statues portraying prophets, bishops, angels and kings. The years have not been kind to them, so some have been replaced and you will find the originals inside the church.

Map 1.1 - Make your way towards the doors to get a better look at the decoration.

Porte Notre Dame (main central door)

Often the main door to a Cathedral is topped with a scary depiction of the Final Judgment, showing good people being welcomed into heaven, and the sinners heading to the flames of hell.

Rouen Cathedral has instead placed a Tree of Jesse above the door.

Tree of Jesse

The purpose of the tree is to illustrate the ancestral link between Jesus and Adam.

Jesse lies at the bottom of the tree, slumbering and dreaming about his family tree. There are a lot of generations involved between Jesus and Adam, so Jesse is used as a focal point since he is named in the bible as a direct descendent of Adam.

The central trunk of the tree shows Jesse's son King David, and finally at the top sits the Virgin Mary and Baby Jesus.

Sadly most of the statues were decapitated during the various religious battles which engulfed France.

Porte Saint-Jean (Left Door)

This doorway tells the story of John the Baptist in two acts.

The bottom level shows us the infamous Dance of Salome, with a very acrobatic Salome dancing on her hands. Next to it is the resulting execution of John the Baptist, and the presentation of his head on a platter.

Flaubert was inspired by this sculpture and he wrote a short story called Hérodias; she was the mother of Salome and it was she who wanted John the Baptist's head.

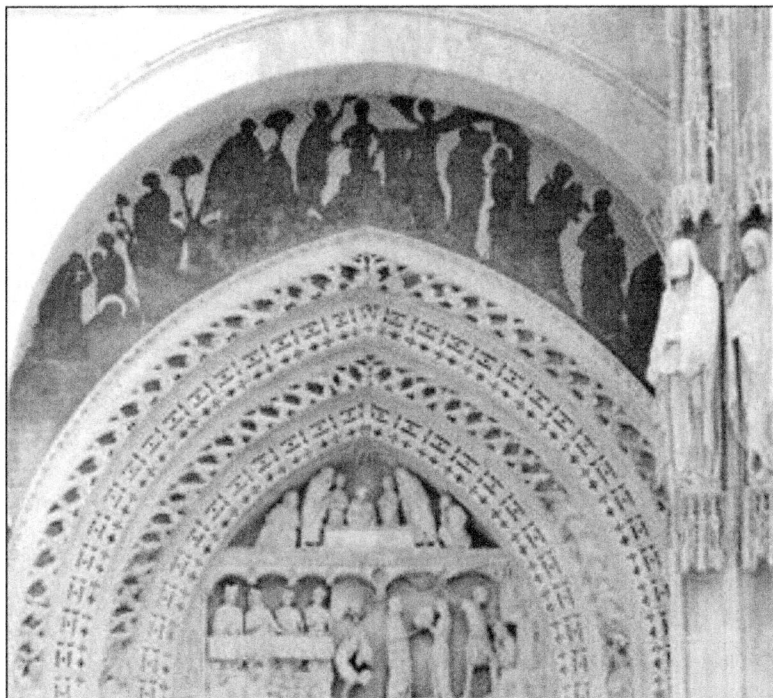

There is one more interesting item on this door which is easy to miss. Above the story of John the Baptist are a couple of carved arches. Above those is an unusual carving; the stone has been cut to produce a dark shadow effect and shows the baptism of Jesus.

Porte Saint-Étienne (Right Door)

The decoration of this door hasn't survived as well as the others. But once again there is a shadow stone cutting above it

If you don't wish to visit the Cathedral, continue from "Leaving the Cathedral" on page 59.

Inside the Cathedral

Enter the Cathedral. Immediately on your left you will find the door to the Baptistery. It is often locked as the Baptistery is only visited when on a guided tour.

However you can look through the gate railings and see the font.

The Font

The baptismal font was only placed here in 1911.

The stone font itself is quite plain, however it is topped by the most wonderfully intricate iron cover. You should be able to see it suspended above the font from the doorway.

The cover was designed and cast by Ferdinand Marrou - remember the name as you will read about him again later.

Now make your way down the nave; enjoy the towering vaults and columns lining the path as you do.

You will reach the transept, where the Lantern Tower rises high above you. Turn left to reach the wonderful Escalier de la Libraire.

Escalier des Libraires

The beautiful stairway was built at the request of the clergy who wanted a shortcut to the library which was on the second floor. Before it was built they had a long walk, as they had to leave the cathedral to reach an external staircase.

The first two flights of stairs were built in the fifteenth century. Three hundred years later in 1788, the top two flights were added to give easy access to the archive which had been installed in a floor above the library.

Keep going and walk around the end of the church. This is where you will find the tombs of the Dukes of Normandy.

Rollo the Viking

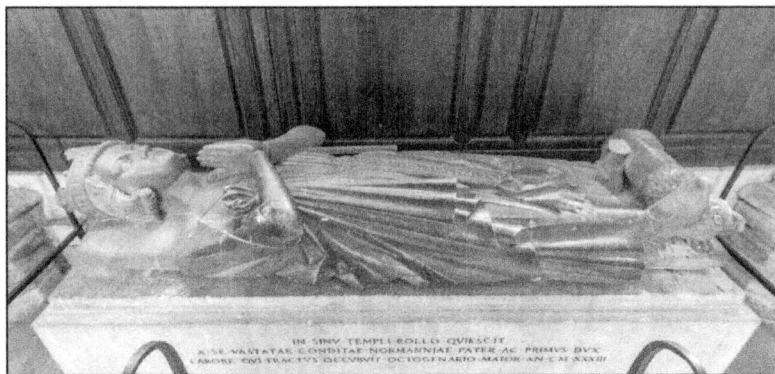

As mentioned in the Potted History, the Vikings who lived in this area eventually signed a peace treaty with the French crown and the Duchy of Normandy was created.

Rollo was the Viking leader at the time and he became the first Duke of Normandy. His remains were transferred into the Cathedral when it was completed. He was the great, great, great, grandfather of William the Conqueror who invaded and conquered England in 1066.

Sadly it's not the original tomb as it was destroyed in WWII.

Richard the Lionheart

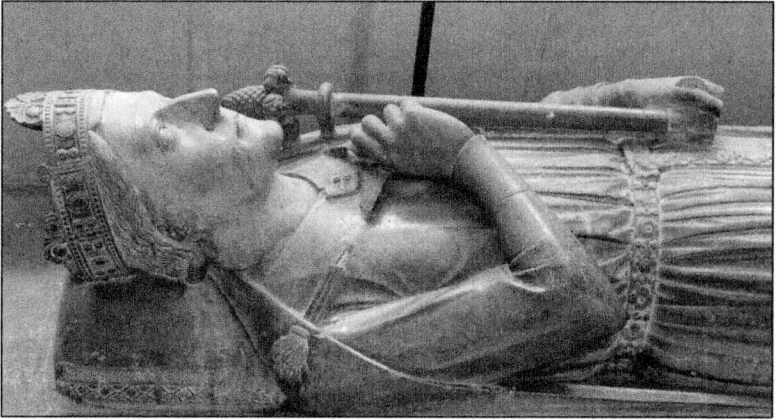

You can also find the tomb which should hold the heart of Richard the LionHeart – as it says on the tomb in Latin.

> This place holds the heart of Richard
> King of England who was named Lionheart
> and died in the year of 1199.

However the lead box which holds whatever is left of his heart has been extracted and is now in the Cathedral Treasury – rather a sad ending I think.

Poor old Richard's remains are well scattered. His heart is here in Rouen, but his entrails are in Châlus where he died (and form a very odd tourist attraction). The rest of his remains are in Fontevrault Abbey.

Hugh of Amiens

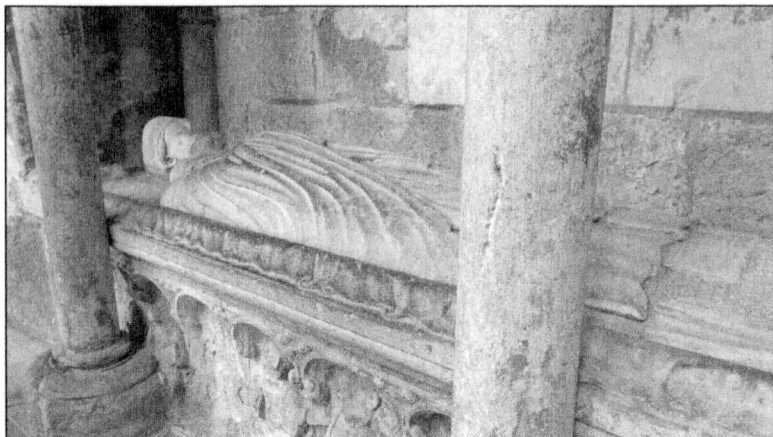

Hugh of Amiens was Archbishop of Rouen. It was he who decided to replace the Romanesque cathedral which stood here, with Rouen's mighty stone Cathedral. So it's only fitting that his tomb is here.

John of Lancaster

You will find only a plaque commemorating John of Lancaster. He is regarded as being the driving force behind Joan of Arc's gruesome death. As a result, his tomb was totally destroyed during the Wars of Religion, and has been replaced with just a plaque.

The Windows

There are many original stained glass windows, complimented by a number of modern windows which replaced the casualties of war.

One of the deep blue windows is thought to have been the inspiration to Rouen's famous son Gustave Flaubert. He ends one of his tales, The Legend of Saint Julian the Hospitaller", by declaring that the story is as told by one of the church windows in his country.

The Crypt
This is another area you can only visit on a tour.

It's the age of the crypt which makes it really interesting. It's the crypt of the original 11th century cathedral which sits beneath the Gothic replacement.

Jeanne d'Arc au Bûcher

Don't miss the cathedral's touching statue of Joan. She is shown chained to the stake and flames licking at her feet and gown.

The sword decorating the plinth Joan is standing on, is thought by some to be Joan's own.

Leaving the Cathedral

Map 1.2 - When you exit the cathedral, walk straight across the square to find the Grande Pharmacie du Centre.

Grande Pharmacie du Centre

It was built in 1925 and is still a working pharmacy. This is one for those who love Art Deco buildings.

The dusky pink façade looks a bit like marble but it's actually pink tiles on top of standard concrete.

The intricate ironwork was designed by Parisian Raymond Subes who was one of the Art Deco period's most famous metalwork artists. His work is sprinkled all over France. He is buried in the famous Pere Lachaise cemetery in Paris.

Look a bit closer at the iron octagons beneath the shop name. The one on the left has the Paschal lamb which is also on Rouen's coat of arms. The other octagonal has the two leopards from Normandy's coat of arms.

Monet's First Studio

Monet visited Rouen and painted Rouen Cathedral many, many times. He tried to catch the colours of the cathedral stone in different weather and times of day and year. In a letter to his wife he wrote:

'I work like a mad man, I cannot stop thinking of anything else but the cathedral'.

He painted the cathedral from three different locations, and an apartment above the pharmacy was his first studio.

Facing the pharmacy, you will see the Old Finance Office on its left.

Old Finance Office

It's the oldest Renaissance building still standing in Rouen. It was built in the early sixteenth century, and was where taxes were gathered.

During the Revolution it became both a prison and a theatre. It was badly damaged in WWII air raids, but it's very ornate facades have been lovingly restored.

Monet's Second Studio

An apartment at the top of this building was the second location used by Monet to paint the cathedral, giving him a more angled view.

The building currently houses the tourist office, and you might want to pick up extra information or tickets while you are here.

Map 1.3 - Face the Old Finance Office and turn left. Walk straight ahead, passing Rue du Petit Salut on your right.

Walk downhill to reach the corner of Rue Grand Pont and Rue aux Ours.

Monet's Third Studio

The building which stands here now is clearly a recently constructed building. On Monet's third visit to Rouen he set up his studio in the old building which once stood near here. It gave him an even more oblique angle to paint from.

If you visit Rouen's Beaux Artes Museum on Walk 4, you will find one of Monet's paintings of the cathedral – it was painted from this third location.

Map 1.4 - Return to the front of the Cathedral.

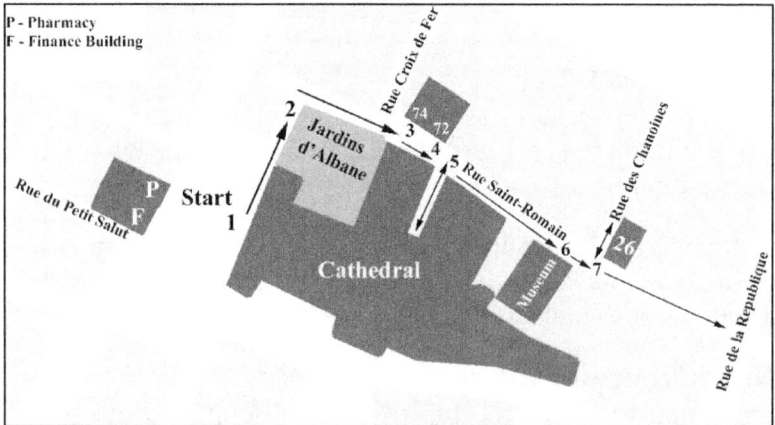

Map 2

Map 2.1 - Facing the Cathedral turn left. Walk past the front of the cathedral to reach the Jardins d'Albane on your right-hand side.

Jardins d'Albane

The gardens were installed to mark the site of some ancient religious foundations which were discovered during excavations in the nineties.

There are remnants of those discoveries scattered around the garden. If it's a hot day you might like to relax on the benches for a break.

The little garden which sits behind a fence is the Cloister Garden. The yew trees were planted to follow the outline of an unfinished cloister from the twelfth century which once stood here.

Map 2.2 – Follow the garden wall by turning right into Rue Saint-Romain.

From here you get a good view of the tall lantern tower which is not so obvious from the front.

Rue Saint Romain

This is actually an old Roman road and it originally lay twelve feet below its current level. It was a major road which ran from Rouen to Paris.

This street has had various names over the centuries, but Rouen finally settled on Rue Saint Romain, after a Bishop of Rouen from the seventh century.

Bishop Romain

A fire-breathing dragon-like monster called La Gargouille roamed the countryside around Rouen, killing and eating any unfortunate who passed by.

The Bishop is said to have captured the monster with the help of one condemned man, who was promised a pardon if they killed the monster. The Bishop used his crucifix to subdue the monster and led it back to Rouen where it was burned.

The monster's head which was used to flames did not burn, so it was put up on the church wall to protect the church from evil spirits. It then rained and the rainwater conveniently ran through the monster's head and away from the church - and so the tradition of embellishing cathedrals with drainpipes disguised as gargoyles was born.

To commemorate the bravery of the Bishop and his helpful convict, the Bishop of Rouen was granted the right to free one condemned prisoner a year, on the day of Ascension. Spoilsport Napoleon put a stop to that tradition when he took power centuries later.

The street has always been a favourite of artists and Pissaro painted it many times. He is quoted as saying:

"If you saw the rue Saint Romain, it's amazing!"

Stroll along Saint Romain passing Rue de la Croix de Fer on your left. Enjoy the old half-timbered houses as you do.

Arts and Crafts

You will find little studios as you stroll down the street. Rouen was a hothouse of ceramic and other arts and crafts, in medieval times and this street was its epi-centre.

The "Escu de Voirre" workshop stood in this street. Its most famous member was Guillaume Barbe who was the master glassmaker to the cathedral.

Pause at number 74 on your left-hand side.

74 Rue Saint Romain

This house has a very elderly wooden façade.

Look up to see the stained glass windows, and six little religious statues decorating this old house. It also has a splendid lion's head on the left hand door.

Map 2.3 - Continue a little further along this lovely old street to reach number 70.

Ferdinand Marrou

This was the studio of Ferdinand Marrou. He designed various pieces of decorative ironwork on Rouen's most famous buildings. If you visited inside the cathedral you have probably already spotted his baptismal font covering.

His most well-known piece is at the top of the central cathedral spire.

Here you can see how Marrou decorated his studio with art nouveau ironworks. On the second floor are two bas-reliefs which show the tools used in making all the wonderful ironwork on display.

At the time of writing it is a very famous cake shop. Do try to fit a visit in. If the upstairs room is open try to grab a table there, as it is very pretty and has the bonus of a great view of the cathedral.

Just opposite number 70 is another old fountain.

Fountaine Saint Romain

At the time of writing, it, like most of Rouen's fountains is sadly dry.

You might be intrigued by the two iron barriers on either side of the fountain. Sad to say, they are there to discourage men from relieving themselves against the fountain!

Map 2.4 – Walk just beyond the fountain where you will find a double gothic gateway on your right. It is topped with intricate stonework.

This is the entrance to the Cour de Librairs. One of the gates is often left open, so pop in for a look.

Cour de Libraires

The Booksellers Courtyard was where traders who wrote, illustrated or traded in books once held business. Before that it was the private route for the priests to get from the cathedral to Rue Saint Romain quickly.

At the far end, you will see the cathedral doors with a typically high pointed arch, and above it is a rose window. Around you on the walls are carvings of monsters, mermaids, harpies and many more fanciful characters.

Slaying the Dragon

One marvellous carving is a handy display on how to dispatch any dragon you might come across.

You must grab it by the ears and pull its head back, use your foot to hold the dragon steady, thrust your sword deep into its throat!

Much less fun is the theory of the academics. They consider that the dragon depicted is actually the sinner which exists in each of us, and which the church teaches us to supress.

The Last Judgement

Above the doorway is a depiction of the Last Judgement.

You can see the line of good people on the way up to heaven, and the line of not-so-lucky bad people heading to hell.

Saint Romain

Best of all though is the statue of Saint Romain himself, who stands between the doors. Saint Romain is accompanied by the fearsome dragon. The rather small dragon has what looks like a leash around his neck, and it does look like the saint is taking his dog for a walk.

Map 2.5 - When you exit, turn right to continue along Rue Saint Romain.

When you pass number 52 on your left you will find another much smaller double doorway on your right. It is the entrance to a Museum about Joan of Arc.

Historial Jeanne d'Arc

This is where Joan of Arc was sentenced to death, and it has been turned into a museum of her life and death. It's a modern museum, with digital and video features trying to immerse you into the period and drama.

You will be given headphones to listen to the stories in English. It takes about an hour and half to get through, so judge if you have time to fit it in.

If you do visit, an added bonus is the view from the top of the tower letting you gaze over Rouen.

Map 2.6 – With the museum door behind you, turn right along Rue Saint Romain once more.

Watch out for a narrow passageway on your left called Rue des Chanoines. It's just before number 26.

Rue des Chanoines

The name translates as the Street of the Canons. It got that name because many of the cathedral's Canons lived in this street, and passed back and forth between it and the cathedral several times a day.

Take a few minutes to venture into this narrow little passageway, as it's full of timber-framed buildings and little gardens, and it's like stepping into the past.

Walk along Rue des Chanoines as far as you feel inclined, then backtrack to return to Rue Saint Romain.

Map 2.7 - Turn left into Rue Saint Romain once again to continue to a crossroads with Rue de la Republique.

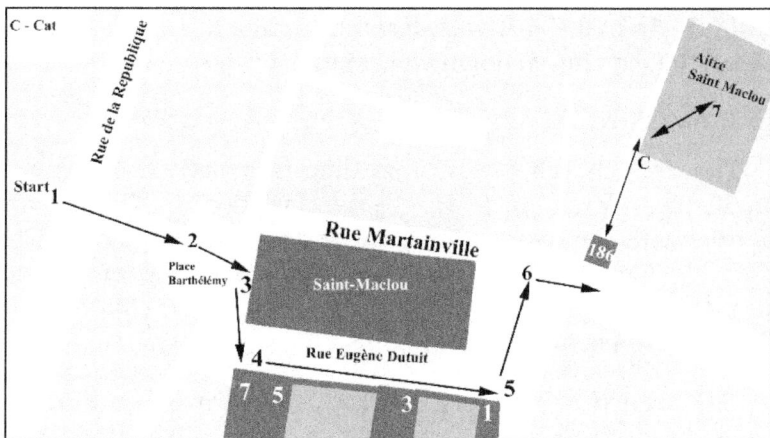

Map 3

Map 3.1 – Carefully cross busy Rue de la Republique and continue straight ahead into Place Barthélémy.

Here you will see the Saint-Maclou church with its very unusual façade.

Saint-Maclou

The Old Church

The first church which stood here was much smaller than the one you see now. It was dedicated to Saint Maclou who is better known as Saint Malo. He was one of the "Seven Founder Saints of Brittany". They were a group of dedicated missionaries from the sixth century who travelled from Wales and Cornwall to convert the locals.

Centuries passed, and by the fourteenth century the old church had to be patched up just to keep it standing.

Finally it did partially collapse. The only part of the church which was still useable could no longer accommodate all the faithful. So in 1436 it was decided to take drastic action - to knock the old church down and rebuild.

The New Church

The new church took a long time to construct but it was finally completed in 1521. It is classified as Flamboyant Gothic, with the usual spires, buttresses, and gargoyles. The church's wealthy parishioners, Rouen's wealthy merchants and traders, were delighted with their new church, and donated money or gifts to embellish it.

The French Revolution, which closed so many of France's churches, at first spared Saint Maclou, but it was closed in the eighteenth century and made into an arms factory. It opened its doors to the faithful again in 1802.

Peace again until World War II when Rouen was heavily damaged. The church was badly damaged and it was not completely restored until 1980.

Place Barthélémy

The square which the church stands on, is lined with colourful Norman half-timbered houses forming a semi-circle around the church. Look to your left to see one which is especially eye-catching; the timbering and windows follow the incline of an internal stairway.

The church which dominates the square originally had a wooden spire, but it burned down in a storm in the eighteenth century. It was eventually decided to replace it by the tall stone spire you see now.

To give the builders enough space to work, it was necessary to demolish the houses which once stood around the front of the church. Once the build was over, that space was reclaimed and named after the architect of the spire, Jacques-Eugène Barthélémy.

A nice touch is the very French rooster at the top of the spire.

Outside Saint Maclou

The church's most eye-catching detail is the very unusual semi-circle of five porches – each one topped with a highly decorated pointed arch.

The Last Judgement

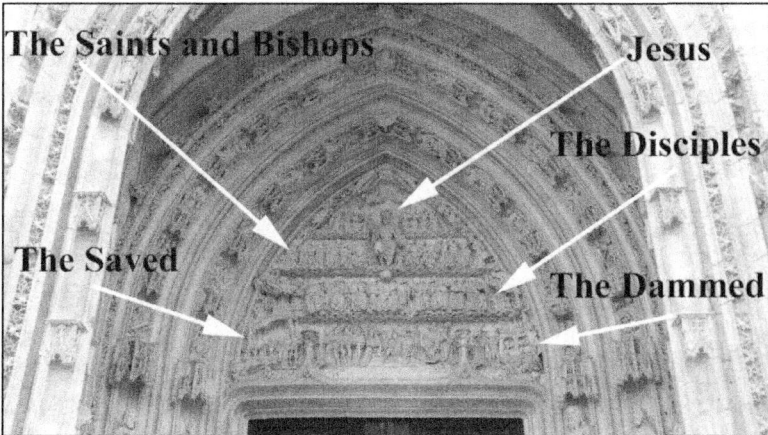

The Saints and Bishops — Jesus — The Disciples — The Saved — The Dammed

Above the central porch is another depiction of the Last Judgment, put there to terrify people into going to church for salvation.

The bottom row of figures depicts The Archangel Michael making a judgement on each soul. He sends the good to his right to ascend to heaven, and those on his left are driven by demons into hell.

The next row of figures are the twelve Disciples, and above them is a line of saints and bishops. Sitting at the top overseeing everything is Jesus.

Rising above the central porch is a depiction of the Holy Trinity; God holds his crucified son for the world to see, and between them is the holy dove.

Even higher stands Saint Maclou himself watching over everything.

The Central Door

Back down at ground level, you can find Matthew, Mark, Luke, and John flanking the central door. You can determine who is who, as three of the saints have their names etched beneath. We can assume the anonymous saint is Matthew.

Map 3.2 - The church is only open at the weekend at the moment. If you have timed it right, pop in to have a look around. Otherwise continue from "Rue Eugène Dutuit" on page 76.

Inside Saint Maclou

The Windows

Inside the church is quite simple in comparison to the exterior but worth a visit. A lot of the stained glass was destroyed during the World War II bombardments, but what could be salvaged was gathered up and later reassembled where possible.

Where the glass has been lost, there are modern replacements which are themselves colourful and interesting. So there is a mixture of old and modern glass, sometimes in the same window!

If you are here on a sunny day you will see it at its best.

One famous window depicts the Tree of Jesse, showing the family relationship between King David and Jesus in vivid blues. Directly above the tree is a particularly lovely rose window showing the Coronation of the Virgin Mary.

The Spiral Staircase

The huge organ was only added in the mid-sixteenth century. To give access to its lofty platform it was decided to make use of a delicate spiral staircase which had originally been part of the rood screen.

Rue Eugène Dutuit

Map 3.3 – Stand with the church door behind you. Turn left and walk around the corner of the church into Rue Eugène Dutuit.

This little street has some lovely quirky buildings running along the side of the cathedral.

First you will find a dark half-timbered house with many ornate wooden carvings decorating it. There is an intriguing little carving to find. It's on the right of the facade, just below the first line of half-timbered "X"s. The little man's legs are running furiously, and it looks to me as though he is carrying a set of bagpipes.

Map 3.4 - Walk along Rue Eugène Dutuit.

Next door is a much brighter orange and white building which has a lovely corner turret, and a garden hidden behind its colourful wall.

Further along at number 3 is a brick building with a white criss-cross pattern inlaid in the bricks. Finally at number 1 stands another brick building with a black criss-cross pattern inlaid in the bricks.

You will reach a T-junction with Rue Molière, which greets you will more lovely half-timbered houses.

Map 3.5 – Turn left along Rue Molière with the back of the church on your left-hand side.

Map 3.6 - Follow the gentle turn of the road into Rue Martainville. You will find a bunch of half-timbered buildings on your left. Spot the opening at number 186 on your left.

This is the entrance to the Aitre Saint Maclou - the word Aitre is old French for cemetery.

Go through the opening and walk along the old passageway. At the end you will walk into a large courtyard.

Saint Maclou Cemetery

This cemetery has been used for burials since the Roman Empire.

The Black Death hit Rouen very badly in 1348 and the number of deaths meant an exponential rise in bodies to be buried. This area became a plague pit, where the rich and the poor were buried together without any ceremony.

The plague returned two hundred years later, and this time it killed two thirds of the population. The pit was needed once more, but it was already full. Christian belief meant the bones already in the pit had to be saved, since you could not be resurrected for the Final Day of Judgement if you had no bones. The result was that many of the bones already in the pit were dug up and placed inside the building which surrounds the courtyard, leaving the pit ready for new arrivals.

In 1780, France introduced a new law banning burials within cities and towns. The bones were mostly moved and buried in another cemetery. Interestingly there was another excavation recently, and there are in fact still many bones under your feet.

The building was then turned into a school for poor boys which lasted until 1907. A girls' boarding school moved in after that but was not a success. The buildings were practically falling down at that point, so Rouen took the site over, restored it, and tourists can now wander around the courtyard.

If you look at the walls of the courtyard you will find all sorts of grisly reminders of the plague pit carved into the woodwork, including skulls, bones, axes, and shovels.

Mummified Cat

One last gruesome item. Near the entrance to the courtyard you can find a window, and behind it is a mummified cat. It is said to have been found inside one of the walls of the building in the 1950s.

One explanation is an old superstition that a black cat embodied the devil, and by walling one up it would prevent the devil from haunting the building.

You will find it difficult to get a good picture of it because the window needs a good clean!

It's a shame really that the atmosphere of this unique place has been lost due to a café, tables, and customers. It would be nice if Rouen could persevere a bit more of its mystique.

Map 3.7 - Make your way back through the passageway to return to Rue Martainville.

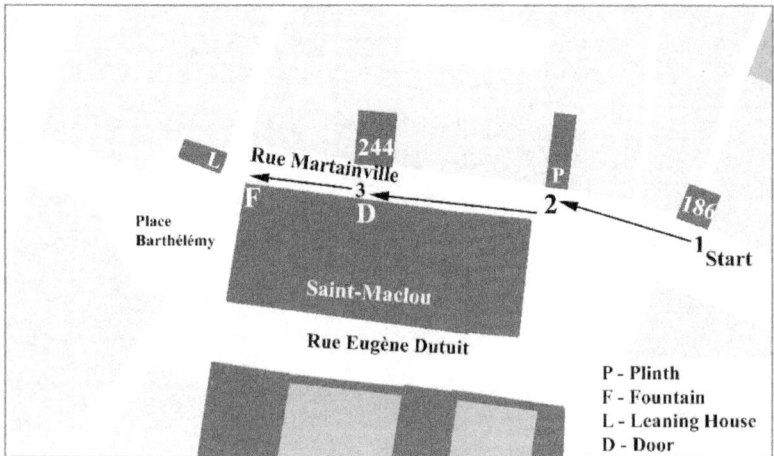

Map 4

Map 4.1 - Turn right to take a few steps along Rue Martainville.

Pause just before you reach the side of the church. On your right-hand side is a building with an iron balcony on the first floor.

Notre Dame de bon Secours

Above the balcony, you can see some cherubs and a golden plinth which is clearly missing a statue. We can guess the Virgin Mary should stand there, as it states on the plinth:

Notre Dame
de bon
Secours
1175

which translates as "Our Lady of Good Hope".

Map 4.2 - Continue along Rue Martainville.

Look up to see the many gargoyles looking down at you as you do.

On your left you will find a beautifully decorated church door which is protected by an iron railing.

The Martainville Door

This door is much better persevered and more interesting than the front doors of the church.

In the centre stands a defaced Virgin Mary. On either side of her is a medallion depicting a famous event from the bible.

The one on the left is from the Old Testament and shows The Ark of the Covenant, which held the tablets given to Moses by God, being carried by the Jews.

The one on the right shows the Dormition of the Virgin, the moment when the Virgin Mary passed away.

Turn right again. You will get a good view of The House That Leans which stands at the end of the street.

The House that leans

The tall building leans to the left, and oddly the windows seem to lean to the right! Don't worry; it has been reinforced to keep it upright.

Map 3.3 - Continue along Rue Martainville to reach the corner of the church. Here you will find the Saint-Maclou Fountain.

Saint-Maclou Fountain

Two naked children stand on both sides and help to fill the fountain by peeing into it – very like the famous Mannekin-Pis in Brussels. The fountain used to have more statues on it, but they have been lost to time and war.

Rouen was watered by five natural springs. This fountain is fed from the Gaalor Spring which flows into the Seine and has been in use since Roman times. Several fountains were built in Rouen to draw clean drinking water from the spring.

The spring rises near the railway station, but these days it is buried beneath the pavement. At least it should be – there have been problems recently due to the spring being accidently plugged by some concrete during nearby construction works. That caused the water to gather and eventually make its way to the surface and resume its path to the Seine above ground.

You have now reached the end of Walk 2.

Walk 3 – A River Walk to the Abbey

This walk takes you along some of Rouen's prettiest streets, then through the park to reach Rouen's second great church, the Saint Ouen Abbey.

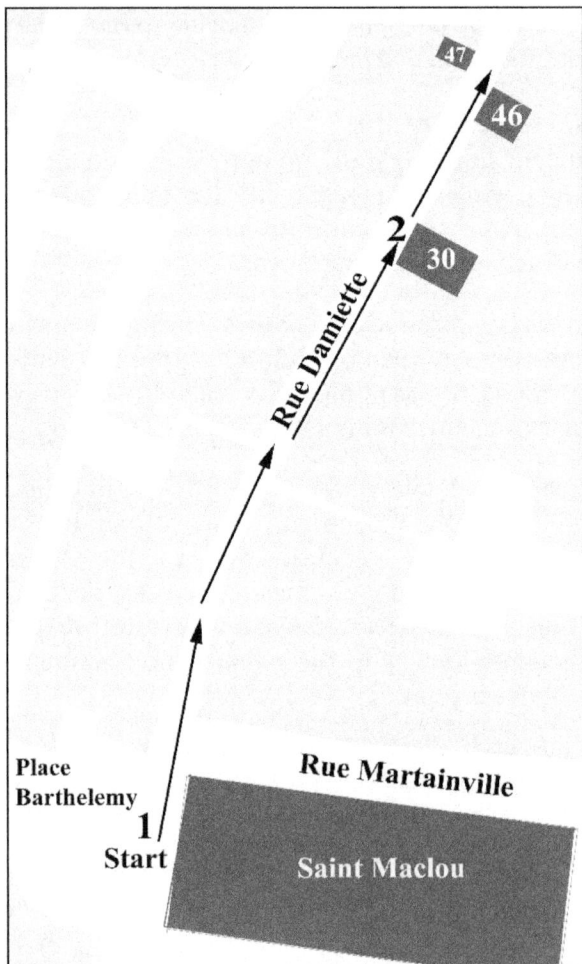

Map 1

This walk starts outside the Saint Maclou church.

Map 1.1 - Face the main door of the church, then turn left to walk into Rue Damiette.

Rue Damiette

This is another of Rouen's loveliest streets, filled with many antique shops in protected timber-framed buildings.

Walk along to reach number 30 on your right.

Hôtel d'Aligre

This mansion was built in the sixteenth century and has always been owned by the wealthy and powerful. However by the mid-twentieth century it had been abandoned and had to be rescued by the city. It has a lovely courtyard behind that gateway, but sadly it's only open to the public on Open Days.

Above the gateway on Rue Damiete is an intriguing carving. It looks like a head devouring another head! In fact it's Hercules wearing the skin (and head) of the Numean Lion, one of the many monsters he defeated while working through his twelve tasks.

Lord Clarendon

The mansion was at one time the home of Lord Clarendon, chief advisor to King Charles I of England. Perhaps his advice wasn't too sound, as King Charles I is the only British monarch ever to have been executed.

After the Restoration when Britain returned to being a monarchy and put Charles II on the throne, Clarendon continued as advisor to the new King. However He eventually fell out of favour and was banished to France.

He settled in Rouen. He made repeated appeals to the king to be allowed to come home, but he was refused and he passed away in this house. He was initially buried in Rouen, but two of his grand-daughters were married to royalty, and they made sure his remains were finally returned to England and placed in Westminster Abbey.

Map 1.2 – Continue past a wonderful clutch of half- timbered houses on both sides.

Pause at number 45 on your left. Opposite stands number 46, which is particularly lovely with decorations on either side of the windows on both the first and second floors.

Have a look at number 47 on your left. The ground floor has an Art Deco façade – which is very unusual in old Rouen.

Map 2.1 – Continue to the end of Rue Damiette where the street opens out into a square.

Pissaro

As you reach the end of Rue Damiette you can see the tower of Saint Ouen Abbey ahead of you.

The artist Pissarro, who trained both Gauguin and Cezanne, painted several views when visiting Rouen. One was from this end of Rue Damiette towards the Abbey.

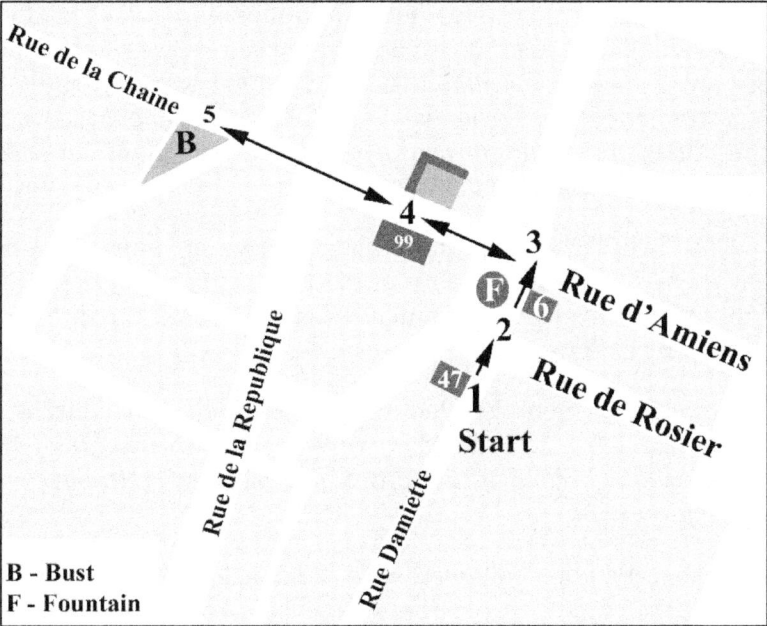

Map 2

Map 2.1 - Walk into Place du Lieutenant Aubert, a pretty square which has a fountain in the middle.

Place du Lieutenant-Aubert

The Conards

This little square was once the epi-centre of the Conard's festival which was held once a year in Rouen.

The Conards were members of the Abbaye des Conards, a group of satirists, poets, and entertainers - the word Conards translates as Assholes.

The Conards led the festivities in Rouen in the days leading up to Lent, when everyone made merry before the restrictions of Lent kicked in. Rouen basically stopped working and the Conards led the revelries with processions and plays. They specialised in making fun of anyone in authority and loved to ridicule cuckolded husbands.

The "brotherhood" gathered gossip from anyone willing to tell them a juicy story. The tales were reported back to the "Abbot" and his cardinals, and it was written all down in the festival records.

Finally the Abbot recalled his brotherhood and a court was assembled. The juicy stories were regaled to the crowd in verse or song, much to the crowd's merriment. No-one was spared.

A huge banquet followed with dancing and entertainment, and a prize was given to the citizen who had done the most idiotic thing in the year.

It's so sad it all came to an end. Cardinal de Richelieu dissolved the brotherhood in 1630 – perhaps the jokes and quips struck too close to home for the good Cardinal.

The Resistance

On a more sombre note, this little square was renamed after a firefighter who not only fought to save lives during the bombardment of Rouen during WWII, but was also a member of the French Resistance.

Roger Aubert helped the allies by sending information on the location of the VI rocket launch sites in Normandy. He was on his way to Nancy to take on a new post in the Resistance when he was caught by a German patrol. He was "interrogated" but refused to reveal anything and was executed.

His last words as he faced death were

"Vive la France"

Map 2.2 - Cross the square to reach a crossroads with Rue d'Amiens.

As you cross the square, take a look at the beautiful old wooden doorway with its two little windows at number 6 on your right.

Map 2.3 - At the crossroads turn left into Rue d'Amiens. Walk along to number 99 on your left.

Hôtel d'Étancourt

The Hôtel d'Étancourt used to stand near the Gros Horloge which you saw on Walk 1. In 1965 it was decided to redevelop the area to house a supermarket. Thankfully the mansion's beautiful facades were carefully removed and reinstalled here on both sides of the street.

The statues represent the gods of Olympus and the four elements. Some of the statues didn't survive the move, and are reproductions.

A personal favourite is the lady on the left side of Rue d'Amiens who is accompanied by a splendid peacock.

Map 2.4 - Continue along Rue d'Amiens to reach a crossroads with Rue de la Republique.

Cross Rue de la Republique carefully, then continue straight ahead into Rue de la Chaîne

You will very quickly reach a little triangular square called Place Saint Amand.

Place Saint Amand

Here you will find a bronze bust of Monet with a splendid beard, sheltering under a tree,

It's only right that Rouen should have a memorial of some sort to Monet, since he spent so much of his time here painting the Cathedral.

Map 2.5 – Backtrack along Rue de la Chaîne and recross Rue de la Republique.

Walk straight ahead along Rue d'Amiens to return to the crossroads with Place du Lieutenant Aubert.

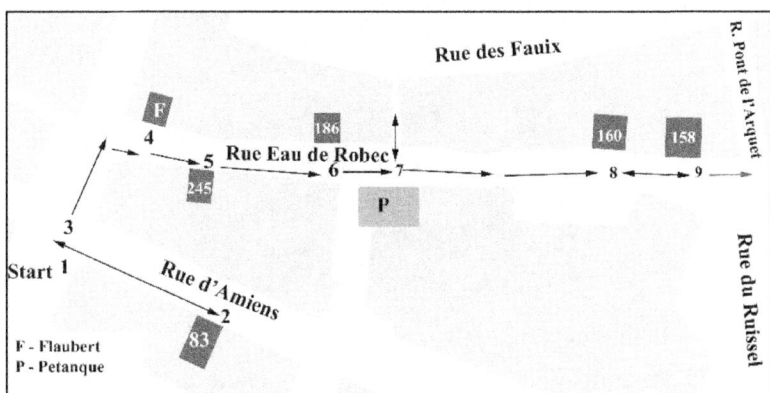

Map 3

Map 3.1 - Walk straight ahead to cross the square. Walk into the other side of Rue d'Ameins. Keep going to number 83 on your right – its only about 50 metres away.

Maison de Bois

This is another lovely old half-timbered building with a really extravagant wooden facade. It dates from the seventeenth century.

At the time of writing it is home to an antique shop, which seems to suit its decoration perfectly.

Map 3.2 - Backtrack to Place du Lieutenant Aubert once more.

Map 3.3 - Turn right to cross the square towards the Saint Ouen Abbey. Take the first street on your right, Rue Eau de Robec.

Stop at the first very elderly half-timbered building on your left.

Gustav Flaubert

It has a long plaque above the ground-floor windows. It was placed there as part of an artwork by street artist Gaspard Lieb. It is said to quote Gustav Flaubert and translates as:

"Drama art is a geometry that is spoken in music. The sublime in Corneille and in Shakespeare has the effect of a rectangle to me. The thought ends at a right angle."

Perhaps you can figure out what Flaubert meant?

Madame Bovary

Gustave Flaubert set part of his infamous tale of Madame Bovary in Rouen. She and her lover hired a carriage, and then spent the day driving around Rouen, paying far more attention to each other than the sights. Flaubert was charged with obscenity when it was published!

His tale does include a mention of the Rue Eau de Robec and the dye-works along its banks:

> The river, that makes of this quarter of Rouen a wretched little Venice, flowed beneath him, between the bridges and the railings, yellow, violet, or blue.
>
> Working men, kneeling on the banks, washed their bare arms in the water. On poles projecting from the attics, skeins of cotton were drying in the air.

Rue Eau de Robec

This is one of Rouen's prettiest little streets and not to be missed. It is lined with half-timbered buildings and it has a little stream running down its length which you will see soon.

Until 1943 the stream was the Robec River, however since then the river has been diverted and the river course we see now is fed from the city's water system – which is easier to control but less romantic.

This street runs eastwards and its length used to be full of water-mills, some of which ground wheat into flour, and others which crushed the raw materials to make expensive dyes. It's said that the water of the Robec regularly changed colour, depending on what dyes were being made.

Map 3.4 - Continue to number 245 on your right where you will find a plaque.

Jean Edouard Adam

It commemorates the birthplace of Jean Edouard Adam, who is probably not someone you have heard of, but think of him when you sip your glass of wine with dinner.

He invented a distillation method which revolutionised wine production in France. He became rich from his invention, but then spent most of his money taking counterfeiters to court, and mostly losing his case.

Map 3.5 – Continue to number 186 on your left.

Number 186

On the first floor you will see an ancient frieze showing us trees, the river, and a riderless horse. It's said to depict a horse returning home after an ambush in the forest where its master was slain.

Map 3.6 – A few more steps will bring you to the visible part of the Robec river, just next to a pétanque court.

You might be lucky and see a game in action. Just opposite the pétanque court and next to number 178, you will see rue du pont codrille

Rue du pont codrille

This is reckoned to be the narrowest street in Rouen - the little alley is only 93 cm wide at its narrowest point. You could squeeze along it a bit to see for yourself just how narrow it is.

Map 3.7 - Continue along Rue Eau de Robec, passing a lovely line of half-timbered houses. Pause when you reach number 160 on your left.

The Little Clock

You will see a board above a passageway which translates as

Come and visit the passage of the little clock

Go into the passageway. It leads to a private courtyard which was opened up to the public to let everyone see Rouen's "other" clock – you have probably already seen its big brother on Walk 1.

This clock is quite a recent addition. It was constructed and put there by the father of the building's current owner, who happened to be a clockmaker. He opened up the passageway to let the public come in and see his creation.

Map 3.8 - A few steps brings you to number 158 on your left

Number 158

Here is the home of one of the master drapers who contributed so much to Rouen's wealth. It's unusual in that the first two floors are constructed of stone rather than just the ground floor. It's also decorated with stone carvings, so this draper was clearly very wealthy.

The upper wooden floors were added in the eighteenth century.

Map 3. 9 - Continue to reach a crossroads with Rue du Pont de l'Arquet on your left and Rue du Ruissel on your right.

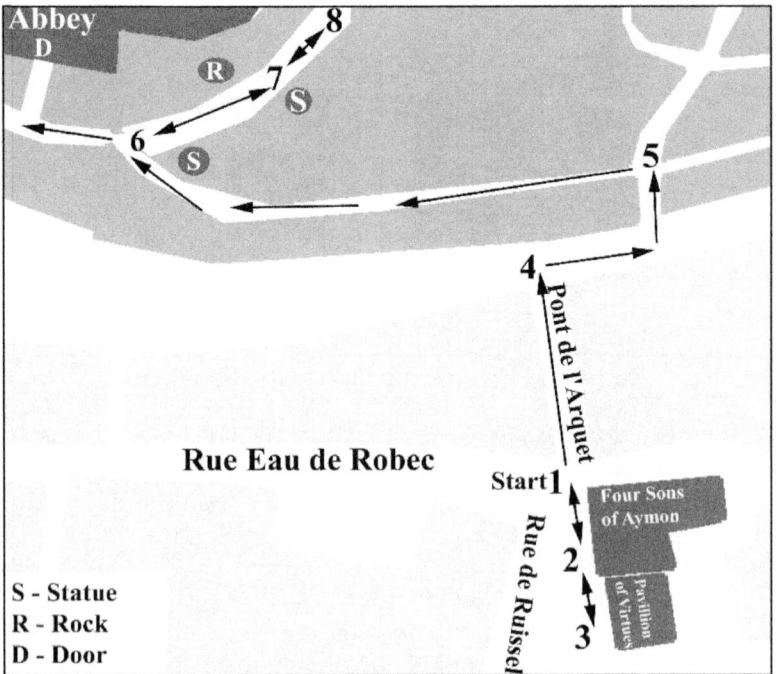

Map 4

Map 4.1 – Turn right into Rue de Ruissel to get the best view of the House of the Four Sons of Aymon, the lovely building which sits on the corner.

House of the Four Sons of Aymon

The building is thought to be one of the most interesting in Rouen, because of the slate tiles used in the construction of the walls.

The building was built by the Capelles family who were another wealthy draper family, and they named it after a popular medieval tale. Oddly there is no depiction of that tale on the building.

The Four Sons of Aymon

Four brothers, Renaud, Guichard, Allard, and Richardet arrived at the court of Emperor Charlemagne. Renaud won the Royal tournament and was awarded a magical horse called Bayard by Emperor Charlemagne.

Unfortunately Renaud then played a game of chess with the Emperor's nephew. The game descended into a deadly fight with Renaud killing his opponent – big mistake!

The brothers fled, and luckily magical Bayard could carry all four of them at once and leap across valleys. Many adventures and narrow escapes later Charlemagne was persuaded to forgive the brothers, on condition that he got his magical horse back, and that Renaud went on a crusade.

Charlemagne ordered that Bayard should be drowned, but Bayard escaped and fled into the forest. Renaud headed off to the Holy Land, and returned a changed man and dedicated his life to building a church. However he was murdered by his fellow workers, but his body was carried by the river back to his three brothers.

The building later became a rather disreputable hotel where bar fights were a regular affair. It also gained the nickname The Wedding Hall due to the many liaisons which took place there. It's said an advertisement from the end of the nineteenth century declared:

Stay the night here. Popular rooms.
First night 50 cents. Second night 20 cents.

The hotel was finally abandoned and thankfully the building was rescued by Rouen in 1960.

The National Museum of Education

The National Museum of Education moved in in 1975. It's free so you could pop in for a quick look round if it interests you.

If you venture in you will find rooms full of school kit and memorabilia dating back as far as the 1500's. It's said to hold over 900,000 items donated from all over France. There is also a reconstruction of a schoolroom from about 1900.

Map 4.2 - Make your way downhill to the next building on Rue de Ruissel.

The Pavillion of Virtues

This façade was originally part of the inner courtyard of another building which used to stand just next door. It was demolished and redeveloped to the modern building you see standing there today. However this old façade was saved and restored here.

It has four lovely columns, and look up at the tiles inlaid into the walls to see a multitude of faces and images.

Map 4.3 – Backtrack to Rue Eau de Robec. Walk straight ahead into Rue du Pont de l'Arquet.

Pont de l'Arquet

There is no sign of it now, but a bridge over the Robec once stood here.

In the middle ages the bridge was in dire need of repair, but since it joined the Abbey grounds to the city, there was a long disagreement over who should pay for the repairs. Eventually the crown coughed up the money.

You will reach a T-junction with Rue St Vivien.

Map 4.4 - Cross Rue St Vivien and enter the park via the gate a few steps on your right. Once in the park, turn left to walk along its edge.

Parc de l'hotel de Ville.

This park encompasses the cemetery of the Saint Ouen Abbey, and it was where Joan of Arc almost met her end. She was tied to a stake in the cemetery, but her courage failed her and she confessed to being a heretic.

It saved her life, but only for a week as she regained her incredible courage and retracted her confession. She met her terrible end in the Place de Vieux Marche which you will have already visited on Walk 1.

As you walk along you will get the best view Abbey and the Crown of Normandy. That's the tall central tower of the Abbey. It gets that name because of its octagonal shape, and the fact that it was the highest church tower in Rouen at the time.

Saint Ouen

John Ruskin was a renowned artist and writer and his drawings are in museums all over Europe. He specialised in intricate detailed sketches of churches and famous buildings.

When he was asked "Which is the loveliest Church in Christendom?" he replied "The glorious Abbey of St Ouen at Rouen".

Saint Ouen's Abbey has had an eventful past. It began as a church in the sixth century on the site where Saint Ouen was buried.

It was plundered by the Vikings who arrived in Northern France in the ninth century. As usual they pillaged and sacked any religious buildings they came across for the treasures they could find inside.

A replacement church was begun in the eleventh century, and sixty years later when it was finished, Saint Ouen's remains were transferred into it. They lay in peace for a couple of centuries but the church caught fire and burned to the ground.

This version of the abbey was started in the fourteenth century, but due to the Hundred Years war it took centuries to complete.

The French Revolution erupted and like most churches, it closed. Napoleon did reopen many churches but not this one. Instead it was used as yet another weapons factory and it never returned to being a church. Today it's an exhibition centre.

Map 4.5 – Continue along the park until you reach the abbey and a junction of paths.

Rollon

You will find a statue of Rollon, first Duke of Normandy, on your right-hand side.

Map 4.6 - Stand face to face with Rollo. Walk along his left-had side to find a large rock near the abbey wall.

Grosse Pierre de Jelling

You will see that the rock is engraved with runes.

It's a granite copy of the original Grosse Pierre de Jelling which is in Denmark. It was erected in 983 by Harald Bluetooth as a memorial to his parents. It reads:

> King Harald has this monument raised in memory of Gorm, his father, and Thyre, his mother.
>
> Harald, the king who subdued all of Denmark and Norway and converted the Danes to Christianity.

This copy was given to Rouen in 1911 by the Carlsberg Foundation in Copenhagen, to mark the millennium of the Duchy of Normandy and its Viking past.

Interestingly, Bluetooth is also the handy tool we use to connect electronic devices. It was invented by Swedish company Ericsson, and they chose Bluetooth as the name because:

"In the same way that King Harald unified his country and brought together Denmark and Norway, Bluetooth connects telecommunications and computers and unifies the devices between them. "

Map 4.7 – A few more steps along the path will bring you to another statue.

Emile Verhaeren

This one is a memorial to Emile Verhaeren who has a very impressive moustache! He was actually a Belgian poet who was nominated for the Nobel Prize for Literature more than once.

He doesn't really have anything to do with Rouen, other than the fact that he died here; he fell under a moving train when trying to get on it.

Map 4.8 – Backtrack to Rollo once more. Face the same direction as Rollo and walk along the side of the Abbey.

Not too far along is the Abbey's second grand doorway, the Marmousets Portal.

Marmousets Portal

Saint Ouen himself stands at the doorway. He became Bishop of Rouen in 641, and around him are bas-reliefs which depict his life and good works.

Note - At the time of writing, the Abbey is in the process of being restored, so you may find scaffolding or other ugly necessities blocking your view of the abbey inside and out.

Visiting the Abbey

Once the restoration is completed, you should find that the tourist entrance to the abbey is this door.

If the abbey is still closed for restoration, or if you don't wish to visit, continue from "Exiting the Abbey" on page 106.

Inside the Abbey

Inside is awe-inspiringly huge. Enjoy the soaring columns, the rib-vaulted ceiling high above you, and the light streaming in through the many original stained glass windows as you walk down the aisle.

Many believe the abbey is more beautiful than its great rival, Rouen Cathedral.

The Organ

The organ sits at one the end of the nave, and is topped with a beautiful rose window. The organ is very famous and thought to be one of the best in France.

The original organ from the seventeenth century, was in a very sorry state by the mid-nineteenth century. Cavaillé-Coll was asked to build a new one in 1851 – he was probably France's most famous organ maker. His only remit was, that he should reuse as much of the old organ as possible, which he did.

When the organ was finished it had to be tested by an official organist and given a stamp of approval. When the organist completed his test, he is quoted as saying that:

"It is worthy of Michelangelo."

The Pulpit

As you walk down the nave you will find the Abbey's suitably impressive pulpit about halfway along, on your left-hand side. It is full of intricate detail.

The Choir

Walk towards the intricate wrought-iron gate which guards the Choir. The choir was where the monks sat, in splendid isolation from the congregation.

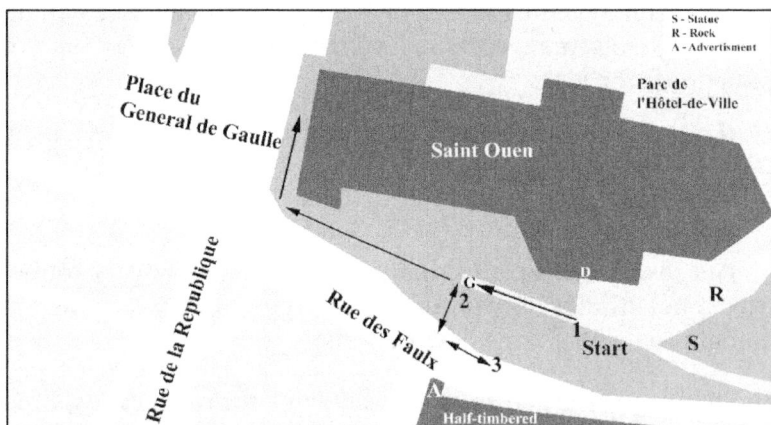

Map 5

Exiting the Abbey

Map 5.1 – Exit and turn right to continue along the side of the abbey. Leave the park by a gate.

Map 5.2 – With the gate behind you, turn left to reach Rue des Faulx. Turn left to take just a few steps along Rue des Faulx.

Rue des Faulx

Rue des Faulx was the boundary between the Abbey Grounds and Rouen.

Here you will spot a lovely collection of old half-timbered houses on the other side of the road.

To the right of the houses is a high building with a very old and rather faded advertisement for Petie Beurre LU-LU biscuits. They were first made by the LU bakery in Nantes in 1846. You can still buy them today.

Map 5.3 – Make your way back to the Abbey, then continue to walk around the Abbey to reach the front.

Front of the Abbey

The eye-catching façade of the church with its two towers and three huge doors is actually a bit of a phoney. It was added in the nineteenth century and modelled on Cologne Cathedral.

You have now reached the end of this walk.

Walk 4 – Town Hall and the Museums

This walk takes you northwards from the Abbey and into the Museum district. You then make your way back to the Old Market Square.

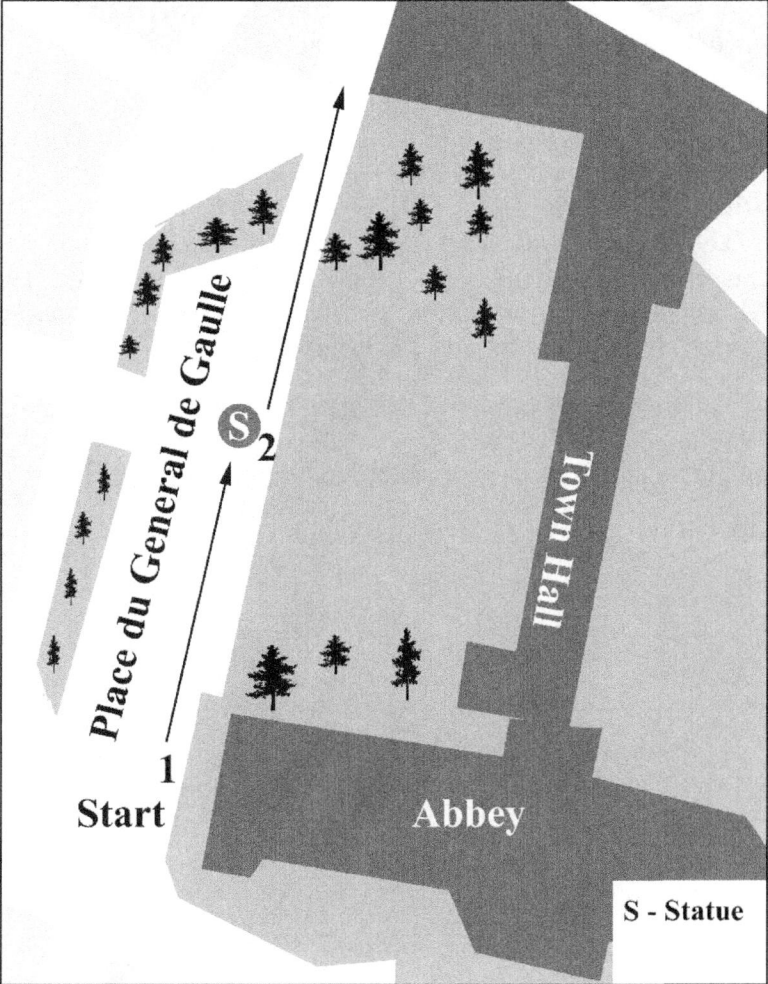

Map 1

This walk starts at the main door of the Saint Ouen Abbey.

Map 6.1 - With the Saint Ouen Abbey doors behind you, turn right to walk into Place du General de Gaulle.

As you do, you will see the Hotel de Ville (Town Hall) running along the side of the square on your right.

Continue until you are about level with the columned central section of the Town Hall.

Hôtel de ville

The building which originally stood where the Town Hall now stands, was where the monks of the abbey slept. The French Revolution put a stop to that of course as the monks were turfed out and the Abbey closed down.

The monks' dormitory was expanded, restored, and turned into the Town Hall. It has not had a happy history though, as it caught fire in 1926 and was later blasted by bombs in WWII.

Napoleon - if he is still there.

If there is an equestrian statue standing beside you, Napoleon has survived. If not, he has been archived as a historical embarrassment.

If the statue is there, you will see that he is holding his famous hat in his right hand. Many people have stated that his hat is much smaller than his head – perhaps that is why he is just carrying it.

The statue was made from enemy cannons which were captured from the battle of Austerlitz, which is thought to have been Napoleon's greatest victory. He defeated the armies of Russia and Austria, giving France military supremacy over Europe for many years.

Much later the statue was in danger of falling down due to rust, so it was dismantled in 2020 for repair. To everyone's surprise a chest was found in the base dating from the nineteenth century. It held some documents which identified the donors who contributed to the statue's construction.

Whilst the statue was being restored, a campaign was launched to put the statue in a cupboard and replace it with a less controversial figure. So who knows who you will find guarding the Square when you visit.

A Visit from Napolean

The statue was erected on Napoleon's birthday in 1865, and commemorates a visit he made to Rouen in 1802. He toured its important textile factories. So if his statue is still standing, look on the back of the plinth to see an engraving commemorating that visit. It translates as:

> The first consul visits the factories of the suburb of Saint-Sever and rewards the oldest worker in the Industry of Rouen
> 2 November 1802

Map 1.2 - Stand beside Napoleon or his replacement. With your back to the Town Hall, turn right to leave the square passing under some shady trees.

Walk into Rue Louis Ricard which goes slightly uphill.

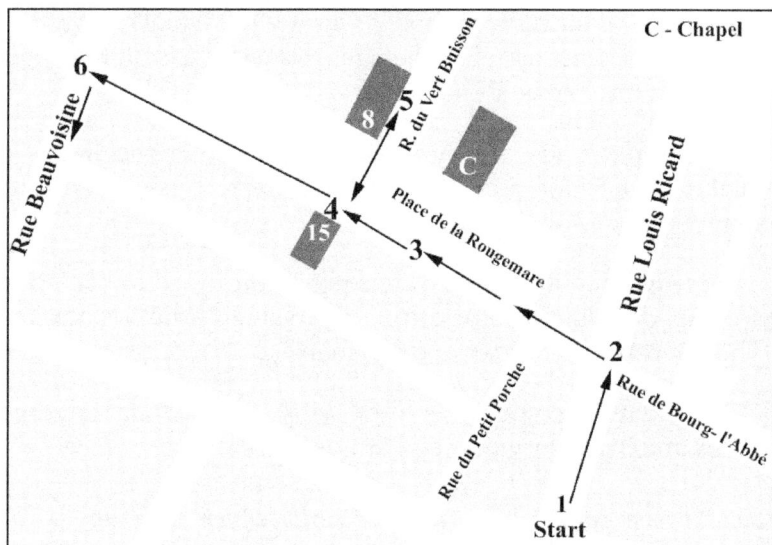

Map 2

Map 2.1 - Walk into Rue Louis Ricard to reach a crossroads with Rue de Bourg- l'Abbé.

Map 2.2 - Turn left along Rue de Bourg- l'Abbé passing Rue du Petit Porche on your left.

A few more steps will bring you into a lovely square which is called Place de la Rougemare.

Place de la Rougemare

In the tenth century this area lay outside the old city wall and was just fields.

It was the site of a battle between the Duke of Normandy and a coalition of the King of Western France and the Count of Flanders. The battle was finally won by the Duke's army but the slaughter was terrible. The square's name is said to reflect the blood which soaked the fields.

It was not until the thirteenth century that the fields of Rougemare became part of Rouen and were safely behind the expanded city walls.

In the eighteenth century the square continued to live up to its name, as this is where cattle were slaughtered for market. It then became the butter and egg market.

These days the square is lined with historic half-timbered houses and has a very peaceful atmosphere.

You will see some steps on your right which lead up to the Chapelle Saint-Louis.

Chapelle Saint-Louis

The building was originally part of a Benedictine priory dedicated to Saint Louis.

The French Revolution closed many religious buildings and this was one of them. It was used as a school for many years, but by the late nineteenth century it was in definite danger of falling down.

It was saved by Albert Dupre, an organist from Rouen who put on musical concerts to gather together enough funds to make the building safe. It was then used for various non-religious purposes before becoming the Rougemare Theatre in 1991.

Map 2.3 – Continue to walk along the square to reach number 15 on your left. Turn to stand with number 15 directly behind you.

On the other side of the square you will see le Vieux Logi, which is number 8 on the corner of Rue du Vert Buisson.

It stands out from the other buildings by its reddish colouring and its steeple roof.

Map 2.4 – Walk across the square to get a closer look.

Le Vieux Logis

This half-timbered house was built in 1898 for Charles Morel who was fascinated by gothic art.

It is decorated with many sculpted figures and faces which peer down on you.

Right at the top is a conventional statue of Mary and Child. But much more interesting is the hunched figure at the corner.

He is holding his head at a rather disturbing angle, as well as supporting the rest of the building with just one hand.

Take a few steps into Rue du Vert Buisson.

You will find that the carpenter, Ernest Villette, etched his name into the wood. On the same side but on the first floor and on either side of a window are two heads, thought to be the owner and his wife.

There is also a plaque on the corner which commemorates the battle which gave the square its name.

> This square was named Rouge Mare
> in memory of the bloody battle fought and the victory won by
> Richard the Fearless, Duke of Normandy in 953
> over the coalition armies of Louis d'Outremer
> and Othon Emperor of Germany

Map 2.5 - Return to number 15 on Place de la Rougemare.

Facing number 15, turn right and walk into a narrow street to leave the square and reach a crossroads.

Map 2.6 – Turn left into Rue Beauvoisine.

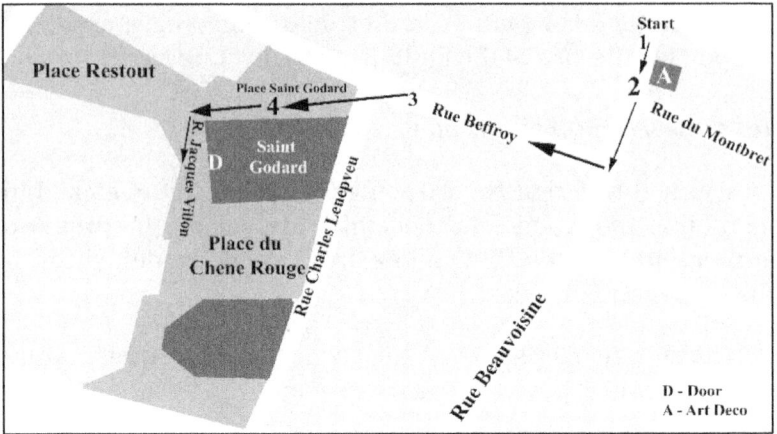

Map 3

Rue Beauvoisine and the Romans

As mentioned in the Potted History, Rouen was at one time an important Roman Town.

As in all Roman towns the buildings were built on a grid, and the town always had a North-South main road called the Cardo, and an East-West main road called the Decumanus. The Rue Beauvoisine was part of the Cardo, and therefore one of the main streets of Roman Rouen.

Map 3.1 - Just before you reach Rue du Montbret on your left, spot the little shop with the beautiful old Art Deco façade.

It used to be a very popular butcher called Boucherie Capron, as it states above the door. Sadly at the time of writing it is being used as a tattoo parlour!

Map 3.2 - Pass Rue du Montbret and then take the next right into Rue Beffoy.

Map 3.3 - Walk straight ahead into Place Saint Godard

There is a pleasant little garden with more welcome benches if needed. The Saint Godard church lines one side of the little square; you can see the multitude of stained glass windows.

Map 3.4 – When you are ready to move on, walk over to face the side of the church.

Turn right to walk along its length, then at the crossroads turn left into Rue Jacques Villon.

You will find the church door on your left.

Saint Godard

Chateau Bouvreuil was built by the French crown in the thirteenth century, after defeating the Duke of Normandy.

The castle stood outside the old town walls and Saint Godard was nearby, so it became the church of the castle residents. They gave generously to decorate and maintain it, and the church became rich enough to install two organs by Cavaillé-Coll who you read about earlier.

Interior

If the church is open you could pop in for a look around. Admire the mighty oak beams which brace the church walls above you.

The church's highlight is its stained glass windows, some dating from the 16th century including yet another Tree of Jesse.

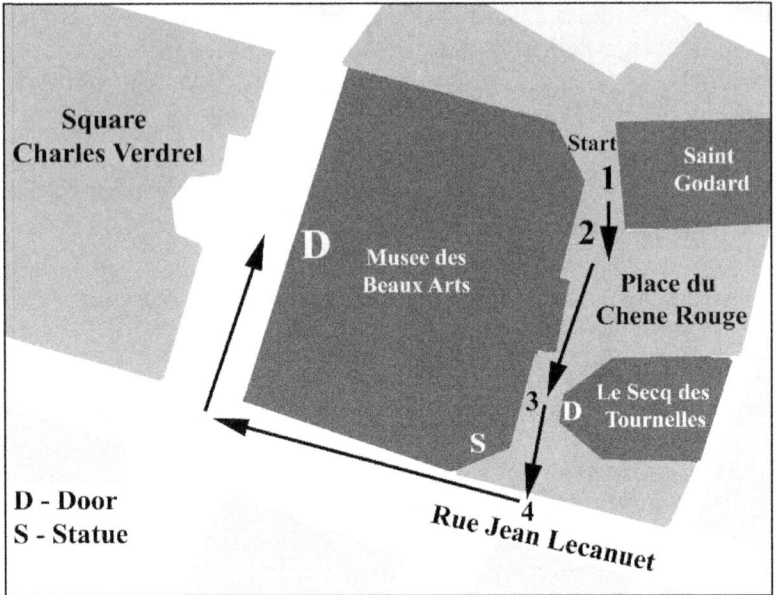

Map 4

Map 4.1 – With the door of Saint Godard behind you, turn left to walk into another square which is called Place du Chene Rouge.

On the opposite side of the square, you will see what used to be another church.

Map 4.2 - Keep to the right-hand side of Place du Chene Rouge to reach the church door.

The church is now home to the Musée Le Secq des Tournelles. It's free so you might want to visit it. If not, continue from "Leave the Museum" on page 121.

Musée Le Secq des Tournelles

The museum is named after Henri Le Secq des Tournelles, who donated his collection of wrought ironworks to Rouen in 1917. It had been started by his father Jean-Louis-Henri Le Secq Des Tournelles who had been a famous Parisian Photographer.

The exhibits are on two floors and it doesn't take long to walk round. It is actually much more interesting than it sounds. The display of gleaming heavy ironworks against the old stone of the church somehow just works.

The collection holds wrought iron items of all kinds; keys, swords, tools, and many others. There are even beautiful hair combs and other very pretty exhibits.

Leave the Museum

Map 4.3 - Exit the museum onto Rue Jacques Villon. Turn left to reach busy Rue Jean Lecanuet.

On the right-hand corner you will find a fountain and a bust of Louis Bouilhet.

Louis Bouilhet

He was a scientist and writer, but also a schoolfriend of Gustav Flaubert. He didn't achieve the fame of Flaubert, but became Flaubert's mentor and dear friend. He died in Rouen in 1869, and a little later Flaubert wrote:

"When I lost my poor Bouilhet, I lost my midwife,
the man who saw more clearly into my mind than I did myself"

Map 4.4 – Turn right into Rue Jean Lecaneut.

The building on your right-hand side is the Museum of Fine Arts. Walk its length and then turn right to reach its entrance.

If you are not interested in visiting the art museum, continue this walk from "To the Ceramics Museum" on page 132.

Museum of Fine Arts

This museum has many interesting paintings, it is spacious and pleasant to walk around, and it's free. All good.

On the downside, there are no free maps or information leaflets to make use of. Visitors are expected to take a photo of a map in the entrance hall and use that to navigate the museum. Information on the exhibits is also online, so a phone is needed if you want to read about what you are looking at. Not so good!

However it is worth the effort. Here are some favourites to look out for as you explore the collection:

Flagellation of Christ – Caravaggio

This is probably the most famous painting in the museum.

Caravaggio makes great use of light and shadow to emphasise the figure of Christ, with the other two figures made less striking.

The man wearing the hat is actually wielding the whip which was used on Christ, but it has been left out of our sight. Christ leans to the left away from the whip, and the hand about to use that whip is about to descend, which gives the whole painting a sense of motion.

The Impressionists

The museum has a good collection of impressionist paintings by Monet, Renoir, Sisley, and Pissarro.

Rouen Cathedral Grey Weather - Monet

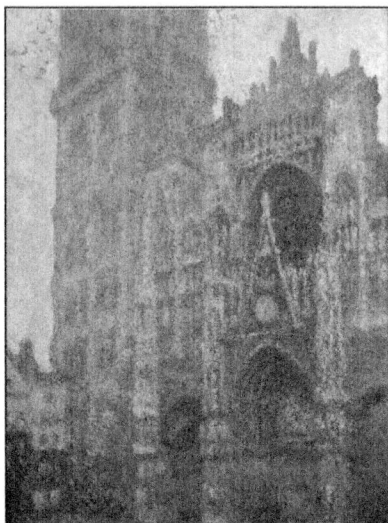

Monet painted Rouen's cathedral over and over again. He wanted to catch the light and the colour of the cathedral in all sorts of weather, and at different times of day.

This version was painted on his third visit to Rouen. It's a shame that it was painted on such a dull day, but perhaps that's the most apt for Northern France. Other versions in Paris and the USA were painted on sunny days and are much more cheerful.

Pont Boieldieu, Rouen, Sunset, Misty Weather – Pissarro

Pissarro also visited Rouen and he painted the view from his hotel window.

This view of the bridge on the Seine and the smoking factories is a much more animated scene than Monet's, but the weather looks just as dismal.

Bouquet of Chrysanthemums in a vase – Renoir

In the same room, and on a much more cheerful note, is the explosion of colour of Renoir's chrysanthemums.

Joan of Arc, Interrogation by Cardinal of Winchester – Delaroche

This painting is all about drama!

Joan is frail and frightened, far from the brave warrior leading her army in defence of the Dauphin. Her tormentor is simply evil, from his posture to his vicious expression. He is pointing to the floor, perhaps telling his victim that she is heading to hell.

Interior of Rosslyn Chapel – Mande Daguerre

Yes, the impressionists did venture to Scotland.

Rosslyn Chapel lies just outside Edinburgh, and has become famous due to its role in Dan Brown's novel The Da Vinci Code.

This painting and other similar works toured around the cities of the United Kingdom in the early nineteenth century, with bagpipe music as an added bonus.

Study of a Dapple Grey – Gericault

We have all heard of Stubbs who is famous for his horse paintings, but I think Gericault gives him a run for his money.

This is a beautiful horse with a full wispy tail and mane, and delicate but muscular legs. His wary eye makes you think he is ready to bolt.

Enigma - Alfred Agache

This artist is well known for painting mysterious and dramatic ladies.

There is no clue as to who she is or why she is dressed so dramatically. She takes her mask off with her right hand, and grasps a blood red poppy with her left. There are more poppies on the floor almost like drops of blood. The Egyptian hieroglyph behind her hints that she is the goddess Isis.

La Belle Zelie – Hubert Robert

I've included this painting just because of the three perfect little curls on her forehead.

The Death of Madame Bovary - Albert Auguste Fourie

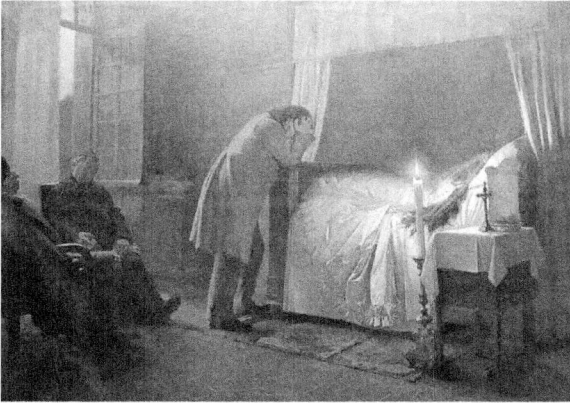

If you have dipped into Flaubert's famous novel, you may be interested to see this depiction of Madame Bovary's end.

Paul Alexandre in front of a glass panel – Amedeo Modigliani

Here Modigliani has painted his great friend Paul Alexandre, in his own inimitable style.

To the Ceramics Museum

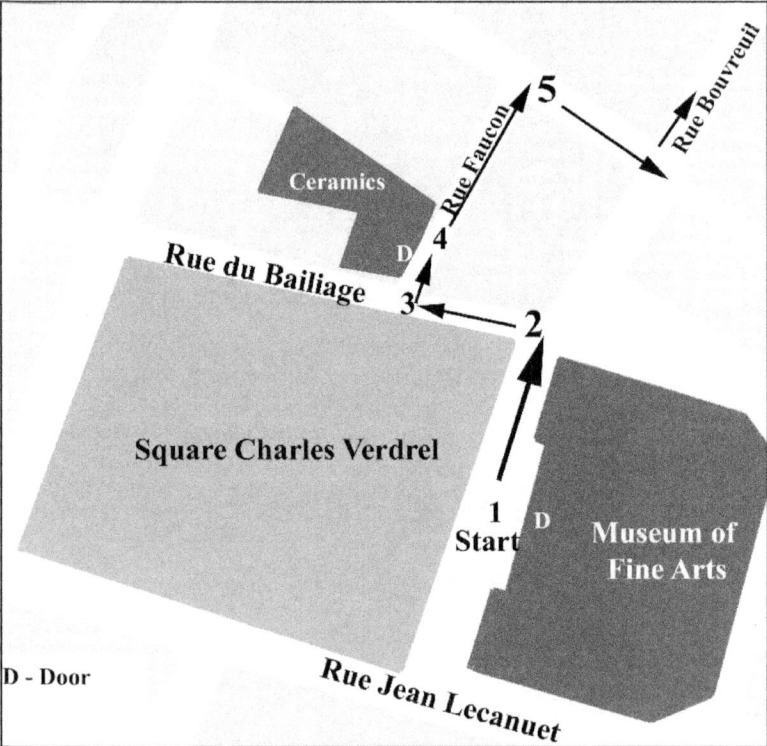

Map 5

Map 5.1 - When you exit the museum you will be looking over Square Charles Verdrel.

Square Verdrel

This area was where the tanners worked in the nineteenth century. The square was crossed by a stream called the

Renelle which had become very polluted by the tanner's workshops; it was a squalid and unsanitary place.

It was turned into a garden in the mid-nineteenth century, and was named the Jardin Solférino after an important battle won by the Napolean III.

It was later renamed after Charles Verdrel, who had been the mayor of Rouen when the garden had been landscaped. Oddly, English had become fashionable in France at that time, so it was named Square Verdrel. Even today though, locals still call it the Jardin Solférino.

The park has had a second, much more recent landscaping to turn it into the park you see today.

Turn right to reach the end of the museum building where you should cross Rue du Bailliage

Map 5.2 – Turn left to walk along Rue du Bailliage. Square Verdrel will now be on your left-hand side.

Continue until you reach Rue Faucon on your right.

Map 5.3 - Climb the steps of Rue Faucon. You will find the door of the Ceramics Museum on your left-hand side.

Ceramics

Rouen was an important centre of pottery production in the seventeenth and eighteenth centuries. This museum celebrates Rouen's ceramics history.

It's free so if you find it open, it's worth a quick look. It does hold over five thousand pieces, so if you are keen on ceramics you might need some time to browse.

If you are not interested in visiting the ceramics museum, continue this walk from "To the Castle" on Page 137.

Museum Courtyard

Even if you are not interested in ceramics, you could pop in to look around the courtyard and garden of the museum. The museum is housed in what was the Hôtel d'Hocqueville which was built over the castle prison.

Don't miss the massive earthenware fruit bowls which have interesting blue bananas.

The Museum

The museum has a vast collection of ceramics from the Rouen region, as well as some pieces from famous pottery regions such as Delft, and even some Italian pieces from the fifteenth century.

If you do go in, here are a few favourites to hunt down as you explore the museum's two floors.

Ruhlmann Vase

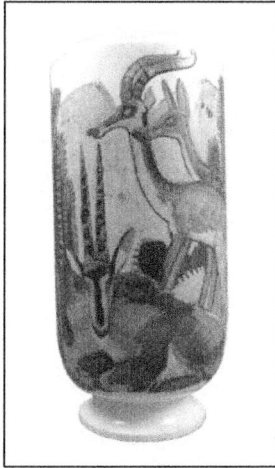

This beautiful vase is relatively modern from 1927; it was part of a seven piece set. The artist took the animals of Africa as his theme, and this vase shows us some beautiful deer and antelope – with one looking directly back at you.

Fennel Coffee Pot

This lovely coffee pot is shaped like a fennel bulb, with the pot showing the overlapping leaves of the fennel bulb.

Delftware violin

This little violin is one of only seven ceramic violins which have survived to today. It's unlike today's violins as the shape of violins changed after Stradivarius, who lengthened the neck of his creations.

To the Castle (remains)

Map 5.4 - Exit the Ceramics Museum and return to Rue Faucon.

With the door to the Museum on your lefthand side, walk straight ahead to reach a T-junction with Rue Morand.

Map 5.5 - Turn right along Rue Morand and then take the first left into Rue Bouvreuil.

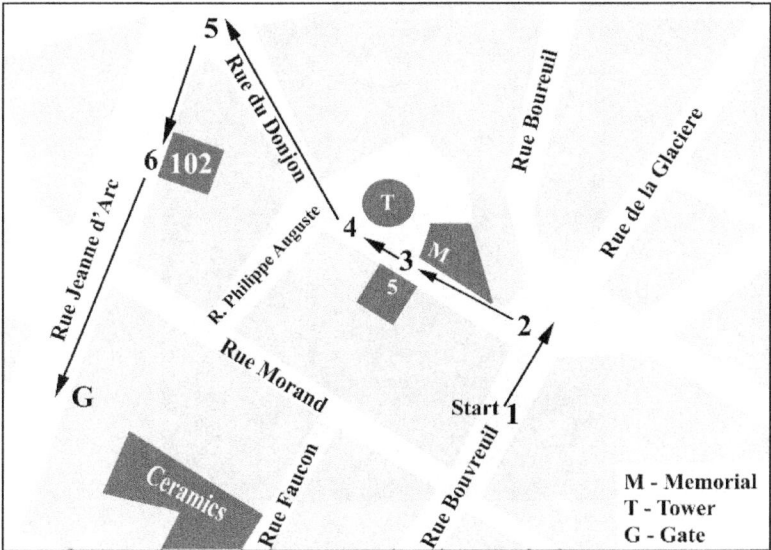

Map 6

Map 6.1 – Continue until you reach a five-way crossroads. Turn left into Rue du Donjon.

Map 6.2 - You will see a turreted tower ahead of you on the right-hand side. Walk towards it, but pause at the corner of the building just before it; it's just opposite number 5 Rue Bourvreuil.

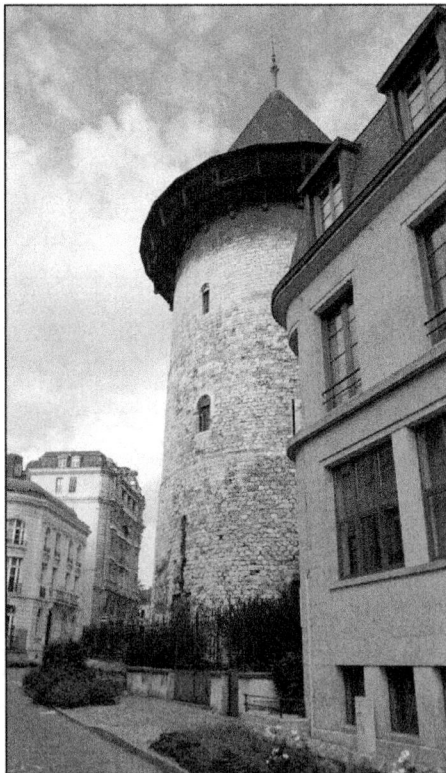

The Gestapo

The building which stood here during the war was the Gestapo headquarters of Normandy.

Captured members of the French Resistance were brought here to be questioned, tortured, and often executed. A plaque was placed on the corner by the National Federation of Deportes and Internal Resistance to the Memory of Heroes.

There is another plaque lower down, dedicated to the Jewish people who were transported from Normandy to the concentration camps of Nazi Germany and never returned. There are often wreaths placed beneath it.

Below the plaque is an urn built into the plinth, it contains ashes from the concentration camps.

Map 6.3 - Now take a look at the tower which stands next to it.

Donjon de Rouen

This massive tower is the last surviving remnant of Rouen's castle. The castle was built by King Philip II once he had defeated the Duke of Normandy, who happened to be King John of England. The castle became the seat of power for the whole Normandy Region.

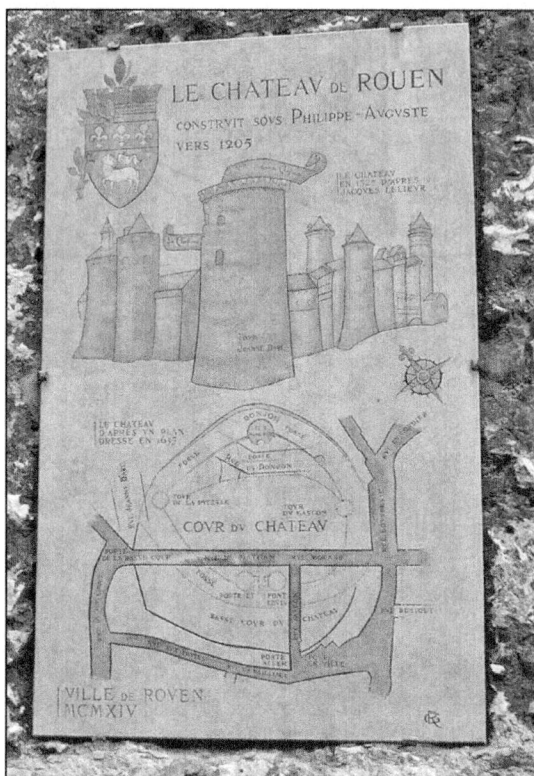

LE CHATEAV DE ROUEN

CONSTRVIT SOVS PHILIPPE-AVGVSTE
VERS 1205

COVR DV CHATEAV

VILLE DE ROVEN
MCMXIV

There is a nice illustration of what the original castle looked like on the side of the tower - it had a total of ten towers.

The distinctive turreted roof you see now was actually added in the late nineteenth century, as part of a popular movement to restore France's medieval buildings.

If you look through the iron fence you can see what is left of the castle moat. A well was also built in the grounds of the tower.

The tower was badly damaged in WWII but has been carefully restored.

It was thought at one point that Joan of Arc was imprisoned in this tower, but she was actually held in the Tour de la Pucelle which you will visit shortly. She was however brought to this tower for questioning.

Joan's inquisitors thoughtfully showed her the instruments they planned to use on her to extract the truth. She is said to have viewed the instruments of torture and replied:

> Truly, if you have to pull my members and my soul from my body, I shall say nothing else; and if I say something to you, I would always say to you afterwards that you made me say it by force.

Unfortunately there is no access into this tower for tourists, as it is currently home to an "Escape Room" attraction.

Map 6.4 - Continue straight ahead along Rue du Donjon, passing Rue Philippe Auguste on your left. You will soon reach a junction with busy Rue Jeanne d'Arc.

Map 6.5 - Turn left to walk down Rue Jeanne d'Arc as far as number 102 on your left.

Tour de la Pucelle
This is where the Tower of the Virgin once stood. It was part of the defences of Rouen castle from the thirteenth century.

It was here that Joan of Arc was imprisoned and tortured before her execution.

Only the foundations of that tower are still standing. The building which now stands here marks the spot with a plaque.

Above the door is a nice bas-relief of the castle which the tower was once part of.

Apart from its connection to Joan of Arc, the building itself is very handsome with its ironwork balconies and its stone foliage decoration decorating the façade.

Map 6.6 - Facing the Tour de la Pucelle, turn right to walk down Rue Jeanne d'Arc. Pass Rue Morand on your left.

Not too far along you will find a stone and iron gateway which is the second entrance to the Ceramics Museum. It gives you another chance to visit if you haven't done so already.

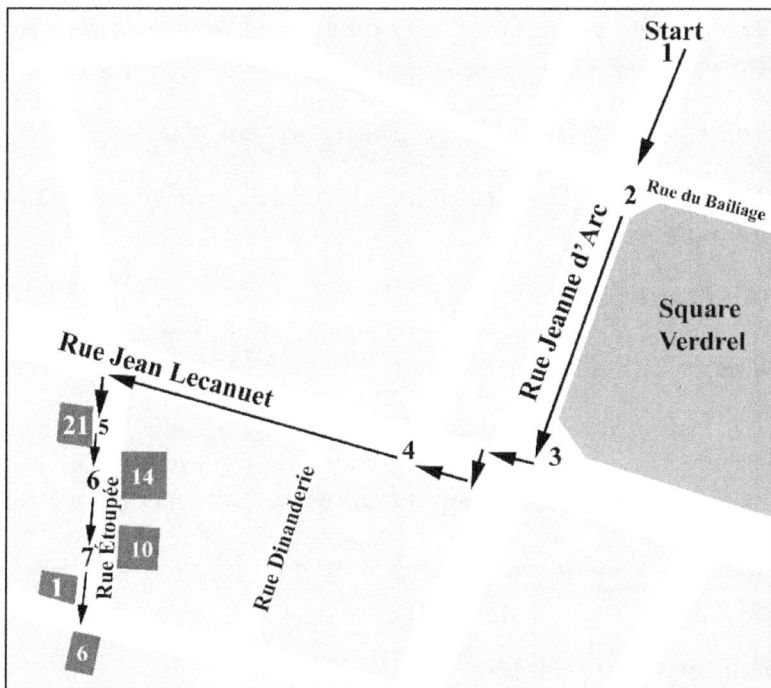

Map 7

Moving on - you have now reached a rather uninteresting part of Rouen, so it's a brisk five minute walk to return to the old streets.

Map 7.1 - Continue down Rue Jeanne d'Arc to cross Rue du Bailiage and reach Square Verdel on your left.

Map 7.2 - Keep going straight ahead to reach the end of the park

Map 7.3 - Here you will find a busy crossroads with Rue Jean Lecanuet. Use the zebra crossings to cross over diagonally right and then walk into Rue Jean Lecanuet.

Mao 7.4 - Pass Rue Dinanderie on your left and then turn left into Rue Étoupée.

Boring bit over!

Map 7.5 - Walk down Rue Étoupée, but pause at number 21 on your right.

Rue Étoupée

This is a nice old street and has many half-timbered houses, Number 21 has an ornate stone doorway.

A little further on your left number 14 is a nice blue half-timbered building. It has two cemented up round windows on the first floor, but the other four above are still open.

Map 7.6 - Walk along to number 10, the fifth building on your left.

The City of Jerusalem

The beautifully restored house is called The City of Jerusalem.

The carving you see on the first floor tell us the story of two brothers who made separate pilgrimages to Jerusalem. Amazingly they reached Jerusalem at the same time, but they entered the city by opposite gates and joyfully met each other in the centre.

The two striding figures are of course the two brothers, heading for the city of Jerusalem which sits between them.

The brothers are sculpted in such detail, from the trees they are walking past, to the wind blowing the cape of the brother on the right.

Map 7.7 – Continue to number 1 near the end of Rue Étoupée.

Here you will find some pretty blue flowers above the windows and the door.

A few more steps will bring you to the T-junction with Rue des Bons Enfants.

Rue des Bons Enfants

This is another street with many interesting half-timbered houses.

The building directly in front of you at number 6 Rue des Bons Enfants has an intriguing little cone-shaped roof on the first floor. It's a niche where one of Rouen's lost statues would once have stood.

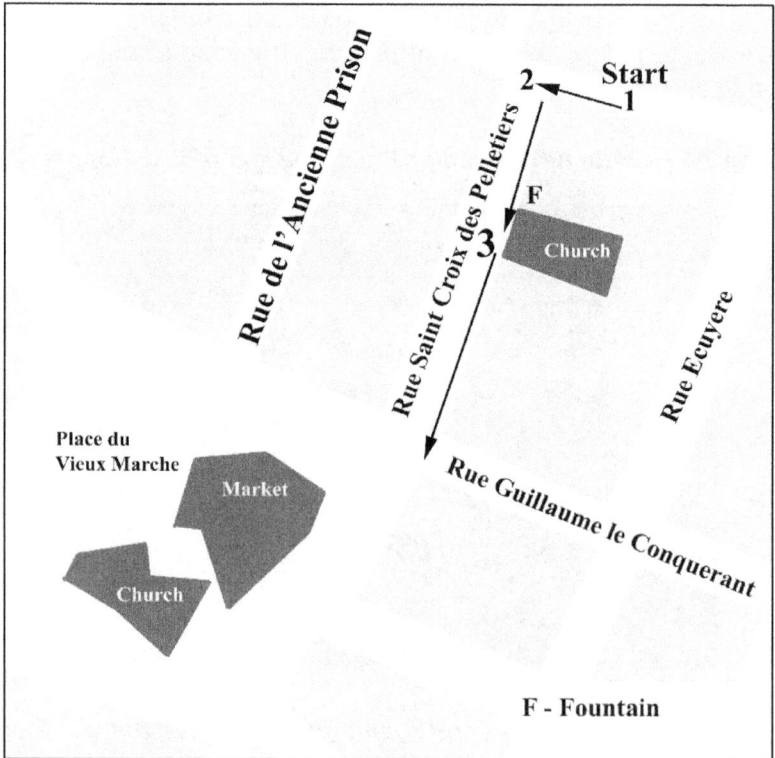

Map 8

Map 8.1 - Turn right to walk along Rue des Bons Enfants.

Map 8.2 – Take the first left into Rue Sainte-Croix-des-Pelletiers.

Just before you reach a church on your left you will see the Fontaine Saint-Croix des Pelletiers.

Fontaine Sainte-Croix-des-Pelletiers

It's a very old water fountain but sadly not working anymore, and at the time of writing is in desperate need of restoration. There are plans but so far no action.

The fountain was built at the request of the church of Sainte-Croix-des-Pelletiers parishioners which sits just next door. It was fed from the Gaalor spring, which rises near the train station and flows south into the Seine.

If you look carefully you will see two lambs' heads looking at each other near the top of the fountain. The Rouen coat of arms includes a lamb.

Just next door is the Sainte-Croix-des-Pelletiers church.

Sainte-Croix-des-Pelletiers church

A pelletier was someone who worked with furs and animal skins. This area was where they worked and this was their church. However the church lost its religious role during the French Revolution and it never regained it. It became amongst other things, a warehouse and a theatre.

Don't miss the odd little building attached to the church, just to the right of the door. It was used by the church's "public writer" who would write documents or letters for parishioners who were unable to read and write.

Map 8.3 – Continue along this little street to return to Place du Vieux Marché, where you started Walk 1.

Did you Enjoy these Walks?

I do hope you found these walks both fun and interesting, and I would love feedback. If you have any comments, either good or bad, please review this book

You could also drop me a line on my amazon web page.

Other Strolling Around Books to Try

Strolling Around Amsterdam
Strolling Around Arles
Strolling Around Antwerp
Strolling Around Bath
Strolling Around Berlin
Strolling Around Bilbao
Strolling Around Bruges
Strolling Around Delft
Strolling Around Florence
Strolling Around Ghent
Strolling Around Jerez
Strolling Around Lisbon
Strolling Around Ljubljana
Strolling Around Lucca
Strolling Around Madrid
Strolling Around Palma
Strolling Around Pisa
Strolling Around Porto
Strolling Around Rouen
Strolling Around Sienna
Strolling Around Toledo
Strolling Around The Hague
Strolling Around Verona

Printed in Dunstable, United Kingdom

65546103R00087